Gluten-Free
Slow Cooking

Gluten-Free
Slow Cooking

Over 250 Recipes of Wheat-Free Wonders
for the Electric Slow Cooker

Ellen Brown

CIDER MILL PRESS

BOOK
PUBLISHERS

Kennebunkport, Maine

13-Digit ISBN: 978-1604332636
10-Digit ISBN: 1604332638

This book may be ordered by mail from the publisher. Please include $3.95 for postage and handling.
Please support your local bookseller first!

Books published by Cider Mill Press Book Publishers are available at special discounts for bulk purchases in the United States by corporations, institutions, and other organizations. For more information, please contact the publisher.

Cider Mill Press Book Publishers
"Where good books are ready for press"
12 Port Farm Road
Kennebunkport, Maine 04046

Visit us on the Web!
www.cidermillpress.com

Design by Alicia Freile, Tango Media
Typography: Chaparral Pro, Helvetica Neue and Voluta

Front cover image copyright shyshak roman. Interior images copyright page 10, Robyn Mackenzie; page 11, Hana Sichyngrová; page 14, Robyn Mackenzie; page 16, Pakhnyushcha; page 20, mythja; page 22, svry; page 28, hd connelly; page 30, Brett Mulcahy; page 32, Monkey Business Images; page 34, Denis Kichatof; page 36, ER_09; page 38, nito; page 40, msheldrake; page 42, Lana Langlois; page 44, Dan Kaplan; page 46, piyato; page 48, Sharon Day; page 50, Patricia Hofmeester; page 52, iNoppadol; page 54, Norman Chan; page 58, William Berry; page 60, Monkey Business Images; page 62, Viktor1; page 66, fotographic1980; page 68, David P. Smith; page 70, highviews; page 72, Anna Hoychuk; page 74, Lilyana Vynogradova; page 76, Brian Weed; page 78, IngridHS; page 82, Nayashkova Olga; page 86, Martin Turzak; page 88, Ramon grosso doliera; page 90, Glenn Price; page 94, Aleksandra Duda; page 99, Fedor Kondratenko; page 100, lsantilli; page 102, HLPhoto; page 104, HLPhoto; page 108, REDAV; page 110, David Anderson; page 112, Elzbieta Sekowska; page 114, Olga Lyubkina; page 116, HLPhoto; page 122, Lulu Durand; page 124, hd connelly; page 126, HLPhoto; page 128, straga; page 130, 29september; page 132, Ildi Papp; page 134, Nathalie Speliers Ufermann; page 136, Patryk Kosmider; page 138, Jump Photography; page 142, Silvia Bogdanski; page 144, Monkey Business Images; page 146, stocknadia; page 148, shyshak roman; page 152, Madlen; page 154, Monkey Business Images; page 156, tacar; page 158, Maksim Toome; page 160, David P. Smith; page 162, Ingrid Balabanova; page 164, Darren Brode; page 166, Joe Gough; page 168, Robyn Mackenzie; page 170, Elzbieta Sekowska page 172, Mariya Volik; page 174, Paul_Brighton; page 178, jreika; page 182, Martin Turzak; page 184, Anna Hoychuk; page 186, Oliver Suckling; page 188, Alexander Bark; page 193, joanna wnuk; page 195 Madlen; page 196, marco mayer; page 198, Francesco83; page 200, Anna Hoychuk; page 202, Roman Sigaev; page 204, svry; page 206, Marie C Fields; page 208, B.G. Smith; page 210, Barbara Delgado; page 212, CGissemann; page 214, Mona Makela; page 216, Gayvoronskaya_yana; page 218, kostrez; page 220, Elnur; page 222, Anna Hoychuk; page 226, Andrew Horwitz; page 228, Douglas Freer; page 230, Wiktory; page 232, MilousSK; page 236, Ildi Papp; page 238, margouillat photo; page 240, matka_Wariatka; page 242, Paul Binet; page 244, Digivic; page 246, Glenn Price; page 248, Giuseppe Parisi
All used under license from Shutterstock.com

Printed in China

3 4 5 6 7 8 9 0

Contents

This book is dedicated to my dear friend Suzanne Cavedon,
who made me aware of the challenges of enjoying life
on a gluten-free diet.

Preface

There's much chatter in the food community today about "slow food." The phrase was coined at the end of the twentieth century to signify the antithesis of "fast food," and this international movement opposes the standardization of taste and culture. They are against processed foods and believe that "everyone has a fundamental right to the pleasure of good food." And that certainly includes the millions around the world who must exclude gluten from their diet. A protein that acts like a poison in a body is hardly consistent with the principle of pleasurable eating.

There's no better way to enjoy the pleasures of "slow food" than to cook it in a slow cooker. Slow cooking has been around for centuries, even before there were kitchens, or houses for that matter. The first slow cooking was done in pottery, as it is still today. By the fifth century BCE, iron pots holding simmering food were left to cook day and night in the fire's embers.

Although slow cooking was a necessity in the past, today it's a choice. With some advance preparation, busy people like you can enjoy a delicious, homemade meal cooked without anyone around to watch it. That's a freedom not listed in the Bill of Rights, but a freedom it certainly is!

In this particular case, you are also assured that anything you cook from this book will be totally free of gluten. There's freedom in that, too. For some dishes, such as cream soups or Moussaka, I adapted recipes to use gluten-free ingredients, and these are formulations that can be transferred from this book to all of your gluten-free cooking.

Foods compatible with slow cooking are part of all the world's cuisines, and while some of these cuisines incorporate wheat, barley, and rye—the trinity of gluten-containing grains—into dishes, most do not. Meals emerging from your slow cooker reflect a veritable United Nations because the recipes in this book are adapted from authentic dishes from far-flung corners of the earth. You'll find soups from China and stews from Brazil and Hungary. There are vegetarian dishes from India and chicken dishes from France and North Africa.

I've also worked on ways to make cooking easier and more pleasurable as well as free from gluten. You'll find tricks for browning meat under the broiler rather than dirtying a skillet and how to effortlessly make dishes such as polenta and risotto that require laborious stirring when cooked on the stove instead of in the slow cooker.

Back in the early 1970s I received a slow cooker as a wedding present and promptly turned it into a planter because back then all the recipes written for the relatively new appliance called for cans of "Cream of Something" soup and other processed foods. This is my fourth slow cooker cookbook, and I'm adamant that the slow cooker is a tool for the modern cook who uses only fresh ingredients. That's all you'll find here, and all those fresh ingredients are all gluten free.

Happy cooking!

Ellen Brown
Providence, Rhode Island

Introduction

Gluten-Free Living:

Food, Not Pharmacy

*I*t's not easy to follow a gluten-free diet. Wheat flour and contaminated ingredients are all around you. But in reality it's far easier to follow the regimen when you're cooking for yourself at home rather than trusting that restaurants really know what's in their food.

That's where the slow cooker becomes your pal. It does the cooking while you're living life. You go off to work and come home to find the aroma of a wonderful stew or soup. Or you take a walk in the woods and find a luscious dessert awaiting you. And with the range of dishes you'll find in this book, a gluten-free diet is hardly synonymous with deprivation.

Understanding the need to live gluten-free starts with understanding how gluten can cause life-threatening problems if not removed from the diet of those who cannot tolerate it. But the good news is that following a gluten-free diet can mitigate debilitating symptoms and pain in as little as a few months—using food rather than a pharmacy.

Our bodies contain a complex and interlocking system to prevent harm. There is a network of organs, glands, and cell types all dedicated to warding off illness lumped under the heading of the immune system. But sometimes the immune system has been mysteriously programmed incorrectly and attacks healthy cells rather than potentially harmful ones. These maladies are termed *autoimmune diseases.*

Although autoimmune disorders are not fully understood, many medical authorities now accept some causes. The sources of these disorders include viruses, which change the information carried inside the cells, sunlight and other forms of radiation, certain chemicals, and drugs. There is also believed to be a connection to sex hormones, as many more women suffer from autoimmune disorders.

There are more than eighty types of autoimmune disease, including lupus, rheumatoid arthritis, and Graves' disease. Some medical authorities also believe that multiple sclerosis is caused by an autoimmune response. While the aggravating factors in many of these diseases is complex, in the case of celiac disease it is really rather easy. Celiac disease is caused by an autoimmune response to gluten, one of the thirty proteins found in wheat, barley, and rye.

Humans as a species are unable to properly digest the gluten protein. Normal protein digestion involves a complete breakdown of protein into small particles called amino acids that are in turn absorbed by the

small intestine and used by the body as a nutritional source. Those without gluten intolerance don't appear to be affected negatively by the inability to properly digest gluten in the way those with gluten intolerance are.

But for those who are intolerant, the undigested gluten protein gets absorbed into the lining of the small intestine but is not seen by the body as a source of nutrition. To the contrary, the body's immune systems attacks these protein particles as something that needs to be destroyed, in very much the same way as it would attack an invading organism such as a virus, bacterium, or parasite. The attack by the immune system causes inflammation and damage to the small intestine, which prevents it from absorbing the nutrients from food that are important for staying healthy.

Normally, the small intestine is lined with tiny, hair-like projections called *villi* that resemble the deep pile of a plush carpet on a microscopic scale. It is these villi that work to absorb vitamins, minerals, and other nutrients from the food you eat. Without prominent villi, the inner surface of the small intestine becomes less like a plush carpet and more like a tile floor. The body is unable to absorb nutrients necessary for health and growth, resulting in malnutrition.

It is now clear that celiac disease is far more common than doctors once believed. New research reveals that celiac disease may be one of the most common genetic diseases. A federal government study estimates that 1 in every 133 Americans suffers from it. That's more than 3 million people.

The condition is diagnosed by testing for three antibodies—anti-gliadin, anti-endomysial, and anti-tissue transglutaminase—all of which are present when an affected person is exposed to gluten but disappear when the offending grains are no longer consumed.

There are millions more people whose digestive problems don't fall under the strict definition of celiac disease because they do not test positively for the antibodies but who have found that following a gluten-free diet helps them. Rather than terming them gluten-intolerant, they're termed gluten-sensitive. This group could include up to 30 percent of the American population.

When you're watching out for wheat by reading ingredient labels, there are other ways it can be listed. Both kamut and faro are ancient types of wheat, and bulgur is cracked wheat kernels. Also be on the lookout for couscous, which, contrary to popular belief, is a granular pasta made with wheat flour and not a grain. Other ways wheat flour is listed include semolina, farina, and durum. If you see a product with one of these names, it contains gluten.

For this much larger group, eliminating gluten can eliminate symptoms ranging from abdominal pain to osteoporosis and sinus congestion. Gluten sensitivity has also been linked to conditions such as psoriasis, anemia, and asthma.

Following a gluten-free diet is not a temporary measure to ameliorate a condition. It's for life. Eliminating gluten doesn't cause the body to become less sensitive to it. The condition for which the gluten was eliminated can return as soon as gluten is reintroduced to the diet.

The good news is that following a gluten-free diet is easier today than ever before. According to a study released in 2009, the market for gluten-free products grew at a compound annual growth rate of 28 percent from 2004 to 2008, capturing almost $1.6 billion in retail sales during 2008. It's anticipated that by 2012 the market will reach $2.6 billion in sales.

You'll find references in the ingredient lists such as gluten-free pasta and gluten-free bread. These were all but unknown even a decade ago, and they will enrich the gluten-free diet immeasurably in the years to come.

Chapter 1

Slowly Does It:

An Introduction to Slow Cooking and Slow Cookers

*L*uckily for all of us who are "science challenged," it doesn't take a degree in physics to operate a slow cooker. It's about the easiest machine there is on the market. It's certainly far less complicated than an espresso machine or even a waffle maker. In this chapter you'll learn about slow cookers and how to get the best results from them.

In addition to being a book on slow cooker cooking, this book is focused on *gluten-free* cooking. At the end of the chapter are some tips for avoiding contamination from wheat flour, as well as recipes for stocks, which are the foundation for most recipes in the book.

Slow cookers are inexpensive to operate; they use about as much electricity as a 60-watt bulb. They are also as easy to operate as flipping on a light switch.

Slow cookers operate by cooking food using indirect heat at a low temperature for an extended period of time. Here's the difference: Direct heat is the power of a stove burner underneath a pot, while indirect heat is the overall heat that surrounds foods as they bake in the oven.

You can purchase a slow cooker for as little as $20 at a discount store, while the top-of-the-line ones sell for close to $200. They all function in the same simple way; what increases the cost is the "bells and whistles" factors. Slow cookers come in both round and oval shapes but they operate the same regardless of shape.

Food is assembled in a pottery insert that fits inside a metal housing and is topped with a clear lid. The food cooks from the heat generated by the circular heating wires encased between the slow cooker's outer and inner layers of metal. The coils never directly touch the crockery insert. As the element heats, it gently warms the air between the two layers of metal, and it is the hot air that touches the pottery. This construction method eliminates the need for stirring because no part of the pot gets hotter than any other.

On the front of this metal casing is the control knob. All slow cookers have Low and High settings, and most also have a Stay Warm position. Some new machines have a programmable option that enables you to start food on High and then the slow cooker automatically reduces the heat to Low after a programmed time.

Rival introduced the first slow cooker, the Crock-Pot, in 1971, and the introductory slogan remains true more than 35 years later: It "cooks all day while the cook's away." Like such trademarked names as Kleenex for paper tissue or Formica for plastic laminate, Crock-Pot has almost become synonymous with the slow cooker. However, not all slow cookers are Crock-Pots, so the generic term is used in this book.

The largest variation in slow cookers is their size, which range from tiny 1-quart models that are excellent for hot dips and fondue but fairly useless for anything else to gigantic 7-quart models that are excellent for large families and large batches.

All recipes in this book (except for a few fondues in Chapter 9) were written for and tested in a 4- or 5-quart slow cooker; that is what is meant by medium. Either of those sizes makes enough for four to eight people, depending on the recipe.

Slow Cookers and Food Safety

Questions always arise as to the safety of slow cookers. The Food Safety and Inspection Service of the U.S. Department of Agriculture approves slow cooking as a method for safe food preparation. The lengthy cooking and the steam created within the tightly covered pot combine to destroy any bacteria that might be present in the food. But you do have to be careful.

It's far more common for foodborne illness to start with meat, poultry, and seafood than from contaminated fruits and vegetables—recent cantaloupe

> If you want to cook large roasts, brown them under the oven broiler or in a skillet on top of the stove over direct heat before you place them into the slow cooker. This will help the chilled meat heat up faster as well as produce a dish that is more visually appealing. Also, begin with liquid that is boiling.

and spinach problems notwithstanding. That is why it's not wise to cook whole chickens or cuts of meat larger than those specified in the recipes in this book because during slow cooking these large items remain too long in the bacterial "danger zone"—between 40°F and 140°F. It is important that food reaches the higher temperature in less than two hours and remains at more than 140°F for at least 30 minutes.

Getting a jump-start on dinner while you're preparing breakfast may seem like a Herculean task, and it is possible to prep the ingredients destined for the slow cooker the night before—with some limitations. If you cut meat or vegetables in advance, store them separately in the refrigerator and layer them in the slow cooker in the morning. However, do not store the cooker insert in the refrigerator because that will also increase the amount of time it takes to heat the food to a temperature that kills bacteria.

Concern about food safety extends to after a meal is cooked and the leftovers are ready for storage. As long as the temperature remains 140°F or higher, food will stay safe for many hours in the slow cooker. Leftovers, however, should never be refrigerated in the crockery insert because it will take them too long to go through the "danger zone" in the other direction—from hot to cold.

Freeze or refrigerate leftovers in shallow containers within two hours after a dish has finished cooking. Also, food should never be reheated in the slow cooker because it takes too long for chilled food to reheat. Bacteria are a problem on cooked food as well as raw ingredients. The slow cooker can be used to keep food warm—and without the fear of burning it—once it has been reheated on the stove or in the oven.

One of the other concerns about food safety and the slow cooker is if there is a loss of power in the house—especially if you don't know when it occurred in the cooking process. If you're home, and the amount of time was minimal, add it back into your end time. If the time without power increases to more than 30 minutes, finish the food by conventional cooking, adding more liquid, if necessary.

However, if you set the slow cooker before you left for work and realize from electric clocks that power was off for more than an hour, it's best to discard the food, even if it looks done. You have no idea if the power outage occurred before the food passed through the "danger zone." I subscribe to the "better safe than sorry" motto.

> Always thaw food before placing it in the slow cooker to ensure the trip from 40°F to 140°F is accomplished quickly and efficiently. While adding a package of frozen green beans will slow up the cooking, starting with a frozen pot roast or chicken breast will makes it impossible for the low temperature of the slow cooker to accomplish this task.

Slow Cooker Hints

Slow cookers can be perplexing if you're not accustomed to using one. Here are some general tips to help you master slow cooker conundrums:

* Remember that cooking times are wide approximations—within hours rather than minutes! That's because the age or power of a slow cooker as well as the temperature of ingredients must be taken into account. Check the food at the beginning of the stated cooking time, and then gauge if it needs more time, and about how much time. If carrots or cubes of potato are still rock-hard, for example, turn the heat to High if cooking on Low, and realize that you're looking at another hour or so.

* Foods cook faster on the bottom of a slow cooker than at the top because there are more heat coils and they are totally immersed in the simmering liquid.

While in many households slow cookers are banished to the basement when screens replace storm windows during the warmer months, in my kitchen at least one lives on the counter all summer. Running the slow cooker doesn't raise the kitchen temperature by even a degree, and you can be outside enjoying the warm weather while it's cooking away.

* Appliance manufacturers say that slow cookers can be left on either High or Low unattended, but use your own judgment. If you're going to be out of the house all day, it's advisable to cook food on Low. If, on the other hand, you're going to be gone for just a few hours, the food will be safe on High.

* Use leaf versions of dried herbs such as thyme and rosemary rather than ground versions. Ground herbs tend to lose potency during many hours in the slow cooker.

* Don't add dairy products except at the end of the cooking time, as noted in the recipes. They can curdle if cooked for too long.
* Season the dishes with pepper or hot red pepper sauce at the end of the cooking time, because these ingredients can become harsh from too many hours in the pot.
* If you want a sauce to have a more intense flavor, you can reduce the liquid in two ways. If cooking on Low, raise the heat to High, and remove the lid for the last hour of cooking. This will achieve some evaporation of the liquid. Or, remove the liquid either with a bulb baster or strain the liquid from the solids, and reduce them in a saucepan on the stove.

Modern slow cookers heat slightly hotter than those made thirty years ago. The Low setting on a slow cooker is about 200°F while the High setting is close to 300°F. If you have a vintage appliance, it's a good idea to test it to make sure it still has the power to heat food sufficiently. Leave 2 quarts water at room temperature overnight, and then pour the water into the slow cooker in the morning. Heat it on Low for 8 hours. The temperature should be 185°F after 8 hours. Use an instant read thermometer to judge it. If it is lower, any food you cook in this cooker might not pass through the danger zone rapidly enough.

Slow Cooker Cautions

Slow cookers are benign, but they are electrical appliances with all the concomitant hazards of all machines plugged into a live wire. Be careful that the cord is not frayed in any way, and plug the slow cooker into an outlet that is not near the sink.

Here are some tips on how to handle them:

* Never leave a slow cooker plugged in when not in use. It's all too easy to accidentally turn it on and not notice until the crockery insert cracks from overheating with nothing in it.
* Conversely, do not preheat the empty insert while you're preparing the food because the insert could crack when you add the cold food.
* Never submerge the metal casing in water, or fill it with water. While the inside of the metal does occasionally get dirty, you can clean it quite well with an abrasive cleaner, and then wipe it with a damp cloth or paper towel. While it's not aesthetically pleasing to see dirty metal, do remember that food never touches it, so if there are a few drips here and there it's not really important.
* Always remember that the insert is fragile, so don't drop it. But also, don't put a hot insert on a cold counter; that could cause it to break, too. The reverse is also true. While you can use the insert as a casserole in a conventional oven (assuming the lid is glass and not plastic), it cannot be put into a preheated oven if chilled.
* Resist the temptation to look and stir. Every time you take the lid off the slow cooker you need to add 10 minutes of cooking time if cooking on High and 20 minutes if cooking on Low to compensate. Certain recipes in this book, especially those for fish, instruct you to add ingredients during the cooking time. In those cases the heat

loss from opening the pot has been factored in to the total cooking time.

* Always fill a slow cooker between one-half and two-thirds full for food safety as well as proper cooking. A slow cooker should always be at least half-full so it can generate the necessary steam to kill bacteria. You also don't want it more than two-thirds full or the food in the center will not pass through the "danger zone" quickly enough.

* Don't add more liquid to a slow cooker recipe than that specified in the recipe. Even if the food is not submerged in liquid when you start, foods such as meats and vegetables give off liquid as they cook; in the slow cooker, that additional liquid does not evaporate.

High Altitude Adjustment

Rules for slow cooking, along with all other modes of cooking, change when the slow cooker is more than 3,000 feet above sea level. At high altitudes the air is thinner so water boils at a lower temperature and comes to a boil more quickly. The rule is to always cook on High when above 3,000 feet; use the Low setting as a Keep Warm setting.

Other compensations are to reduce the liquid in a recipe by a few tablespoons and add about 5 to 10 percent more cooking time. The liquid may be bubbling, but it's not 212°F at first.

Avoiding Contamination

If you're new to gluten-free cooking, or you're making these dishes for someone who must follow a gluten-free diet, the whole concept of contamination is perhaps new to you as well. Setting up your system so that foods containing gluten and gluten-free foods never meet can take time, but it is time well spent.

Here are some rules to follow to ensure that your gluten-free products are not inadvertently contaminated by wheat flour or any food containing gluten:

* Thoroughly wash cabinets where gluten-free products will be stored, and make sure everyone who uses the kitchen is aware that these cabinets contain only gluten-free food. However, unless the kitchen is to be free of all gluten-containing foods, it's still wise to place gluten-free ingredients in airtight containers before storing them.

* Clean all the kitchen surfaces thoroughly before starting to prepare gluten-free dishes, and then change the dishrag and dishtowel for a fresh one. Don't use a sponge because it cannot be properly cleaned to make it free from gluten. The same is true for porous surfaces such as wooden cutting boards. Have special ones for gluten-free ingredients.

* Have separate containers of butter or margarine for gluten-free cooking. Crumbs from someone's morning toast could have landed on a stick of butter at breakfast.

* Have separate containers of ingredients for all gluten-free cooking. Even though there is no gluten in granulated sugar or salt, molecules of wheat flour could have landed on them.

* Always place the gluten-free foods on the top shelf of the refrigerator to avoid risks of spills on them.

* Foil is a great way to avoid contamination. Use foil to keep foods separate when preparing, cooking, or storing.

∗ Use stickers of different colors when storing gluten-free foods to segregate them from other foods.

Stocking Up

These stocks are referenced in countless recipes in this book. Stocks are no more difficult to make than boiling water; all they are is lots of water into which other ingredients simmer for many hours to create water with an enriched flavor.

In the same way that you can utilize bits of leftover vegetables in soups, many of the vegetables that go into stocks would otherwise end up in the garbage or compost bin. Save those carrot and onion peeling, parsley stems, the base off a celery stalk, and the dark green scallion tops. All those foods might not wend their way into a cooking dish, but they're fine for stock!

I keep different bags in my freezer in anticipation of making stock on a regular basis. There are individual ones for chicken trimmings, beef and veal (but not pork) trimmings, shrimp shells, fish skin and bones, and one for vegetables past their prime and their trimmings. When a bag is full, it's time to make stock.

Once your stock is cooked—and the fat removed from chicken and beef stock—you should freeze it in containers of different sizes. I do about half a batch in heavy, resealable quart bags; they are the basis for soups. Bags take up less room in the freezer than containers. Freeze them flat on a baking sheet and then they can be stacked on a freezer shelf or in the cubbyholes on the freezer door.

I then freeze stock in 1-cup measures and some in ice cube trays. Measure the capacity of your ice cube tray with a measuring tablespoon; it will be somewhere between 1 and 3 tablespoons. Keep a bag of stock cubes for those recipes that require just a small amount.

Chicken Stock

Chicken stock is used more than any other stock. It adds a rich flavor to soups not created when using water, and it is used in recipes for pork and veal as well as poultry. You'll see in the variations at the end of this recipe that there are ways to make it more appropriate to various ethnic cuisines too.

Makes 2 quarts | Prep time: 10 minutes | Minimum cook time: 4 hours in a medium slow cooker

2 quarts boiling water

2 pounds chicken pieces
(bones, skin, wing tips, etc.)

1 carrot, cut into ½-inch chunks

1 medium onion, sliced

1 celery rib, sliced

1 tablespoon black peppercorns

3 parsley sprigs, rinsed

3 thyme sprigs, rinsed, or 1 teaspoon dried

2 garlic cloves, peeled

1 bay leaf

1. Pour water into the slow cooker. Add chicken pieces, carrot, onion, celery, peppercorns, parsley, thyme, garlic, and bay leaf. Cook on Low for 8 to 10 hours or on High for 4 to 5 hours, or until chicken and vegetables are falling apart.

2. Strain stock through a sieve into a mixing bowl. Press down on solids with the back of a spoon to extract as much liquid as possible. Discard solids.

3. Chill stock. Remove and discard fat layer from top. Ladle stock into containers.

Note: The stock can be refrigerated for up to 4 days or frozen for up to 6 months.

Variations:

✳ For Ham Stock, substitute ham bones for the chicken.

✳ Add 3 tablespoons sliced fresh ginger and 4 scallions, white parts and 4 inches of green tops, for Asian Chicken Stock.

✳ Substitute cilantro for the parsley, and add 1 jalapeño or serrano chile and 1 sprig fresh oregano (or 1 teaspoon dried) for Hispanic Chicken Stock.

✳ For browner chicken stock: Preheat the oven broiler, and line a broiler pan with heavy-duty aluminum foil. Broil chicken bones for 3 minutes per side or until browned, and use the browned bones for the stock.

> Starting the time in the slow cooker with the liquid already boiling saves hours of cooking time. This is a tip that can be applied to anything you cook in the slow cooker. To test to see how much time it saves, start a recipe and see how long it takes to come to a boil. That is the amount of time you can save.

Beef Stock

For a long-simmered meat dish, here's your key to delicious flavor. You'll notice that I don't add salt to any of the stocks because they can then be reduced for sauces without becoming salty. This is especially important for beef stock.

Makes 2 quarts | Prep time: 15 minutes | Minimum cook time: 5 hours in a medium slow cooker

2 pounds beef shank or meaty beef bones

2 quarts boiling water

1 carrot, cut into ½-inch chunks

1 medium onion, sliced

1 celery rib, sliced

1 tablespoon black peppercorns

3 parsley sprigs, rinsed

3 thyme sprigs, rinsed, or 1 teaspoon dried

2 garlic cloves, peeled

1 bay leaf

1. Preheat the oven broiler, and line a broiler pan with heavy-duty aluminum foil. Broil beef for 3 minutes per side or until browned. Transfer beef to the slow cooker, and pour in any juices that have collected in the pan.

2. Add water, carrot, onion, celery, peppercorns, parsley, thyme, garlic, and bay leaf. Cook on Low for 10 to 12 hours or on High for 5 to 6 hours, or until meat is very soft.

3. Strain stock through a sieve into a mixing bowl. Press down on solids with the back of a spoon to extract as much liquid as possible. Discard solids.

4. Chill stock. Remove and discard fat layer from top. Ladle stock into containers.

Note: The stock can be refrigerated for up to 4 days or frozen for up to 6 months.

Variation:

✳ Substitute veal shanks or veal breast for the beef for a more delicate Veal Stock.

> If you have gravy from a meat dish remaining when there's no more meat, feel free to add it to the beef stock. It will enrich the flavor.

Vegetable Stock

Even if you're cooking a vegetarian dish, it's important to start with vegetable stock rather than adding more vegetables to the dish. It creates the background for all other flavors.

Makes 2 quarts | *Prep time: 10 minutes* | *Minimum cook time: 3 hours in a medium slow cooker*

2 quarts boiling water

2 carrots, thinly sliced

2 celery ribs, sliced

2 leeks, white parts only, thinly sliced

1 small onion, thinly sliced

1 tablespoon black peppercorns

3 parsley sprigs, rinsed

3 thyme sprigs, rinsed, or 1 tsp. dried

2 garlic cloves, peeled

1 bay leaf

1. Pour water into the slow cooker, and add carrots, celery, leeks, onion, peppercorns, parsley, thyme, garlic, and bay leaf. Cook on Low for 6 to 8 hours or on High for 3 to 4 hours, or until vegetables are soft.

2. Strain stock through a sieve into a mixing bowl. Press down on solids with the back of a spoon to extract as much liquid as possible. Discard solids.

3. Chill stock, and then ladle stock into containers.

Note: The stock can be refrigerated for up to 4 days or frozen for up to 6 months.

Save the water you use when boiling mildly flavored vegetables such as carrots or green beans, and make them part of the liquid used for the stock. However, the water from any member of the cabbage family, like broccoli or cauliflower, is too strong.

There's a reason why bay leaves should always be discarded. Although they add a pungent and woodsy flavor and aroma to dishes, they can be quite a bitter mouthful if you accidentally eat one. That's also why bay leaves are always added whole. If they were broken into pieces, it would be a real scavenger hunt to retrieve them.

Seafood Stock

I prefer using seafood stock to fish stock in recipes because I've found it to be more delicate. If you have a fishmonger nearby who sells cooked lobster meat, they'll either give you the shells or charge you a very modest amount for them.

Makes 2 quarts | Prep time: 10 minutes | Minimum cook time: 4 hours in a medium slow cooker

3 lobster bodies (whole lobsters from which the tail and claw meat has been removed) or 2 lobster bodies and the shells from 2 pounds raw shrimp

2 quarts boiling water

1 cup dry white wine

1 carrot, cut into ½-inch chunks

2 leeks, white parts only, sliced

1 celery rib, sliced

1 tablespoon black peppercorns

3 parsley sprigs, rinsed

3 thyme sprigs, rinsed, or 1 teaspoon dried

3 sprigs fresh tarragon, or 1 teaspoon dried

2 garlic cloves, peeled

1 bay leaf

1. Pull top shell off lobster body. Scrape off and discard feathery gills, then break body into small pieces. Place pieces into the slow cooker, and repeat with remaining lobster bodies. Add shrimp shells, if used.

2. Pour boiling water and wine into the slow cooker, and add carrots, leeks, celery, peppercorns, parsley, thyme, tarragon, garlic, and bay leaf. Cook on Low for 8 to 10 hours or on High for 4 to 5 hours, or until vegetables are soft.

3. Strain stock through a sieve into a mixing bowl. Press down on solids with the back of a spoon to extract as much liquid as possible. Discard solids.

4. Chill stock, and then ladle stock into containers.

Note: The stock can be refrigerated for up to 4 days or frozen for up to 6 months.

Variation:

✳ Substitute 1½ pounds fish trimmings such as skin, bones, and heads from any firm-fleshed white fish like snapper or cod for the shellfish for Fish Stock.

Although there are now a lot of commercial fish and seafood stocks on the market, in a pinch you can also substitute diluted bottled clam juice. Use a proportion of two-thirds clam juice to one-third water.

Chapter 2

Small Soups as Starters

*S*oups are appropriate for any time of the year, and they are a great first course because they can be totally done in advance, allowing you to concentrate on last-minute preparations for other parts of the meal. Most people on gluten-free diets shy away from ordering soups in restaurants because so many of them are thickened with a roux made with wheat flour. But there are no worries when cooking the delectable range of recipes in this chapter.

Some of the soups are thick and have a creamy texture from the pureeing of vegetables, while others are made with cream itself. When making cream soups in a slow cooker, the cream is added just before the cooking time is over because cream does not fare well with many hours of cooking.

I developed the recipes for the vegetable soups in this chapter with chicken stock, because I believe it adds a richness not found in vegetable stock. However, feel free to substitute vegetable stock to make these recipes vegetarian; you'll find the recipe on page 24. After a cornucopia of both hot and chilled vegetable soups you'll find many featuring seafood. I still subscribe to the white wine before red wine rule; white wines are poured with fish and seafood while red wines accompany the meats that follow. And then the chapter ends with some soups made with poultry and meat, including some of my Asian favorites.

Asian Acorn Squash Bisque

There are forms of what we term winter squash grown in Asia too, so I wanted to create a Fusion Cuisine approach to this fall classic soup. The use of hoisin sauce and Chinese five-spice powder creates a soup with complexity.

Makes 6 to 8 servings | Prep time: 15 minutes | Minimum cook time: 3½ hours in a medium slow cooker

3½ pounds acorn squash, peeled and cut into 1-inch chunks

3 cups Chicken Stock (page 21) or purchased stock

⅓ cup hoisin sauce

¼ cup sweet sherry

2 tablespoons chopped fresh cilantro

½ teaspoon Chinese five-spice powder

1 cup half-and-half

Salt and freshly ground black pepper to taste

1. Place squash, stock, hoisin sauce, sherry, cilantro, and five-spice powder in the slow cooker, and stir well. Cook on Low for 6 to 8 hours or on High for 3 to 4 hours, or until squash is tender.

2. If cooking on Low, raise the heat to High. Add half-and-half, and cook soup for an additional 10 to 20 minutes, or until simmering. Allow soup to cool for 10 minutes. Either puree it with an immersion blender, or strain solids from soup and puree them in a food processor fitted with the steel blade or in a blender, and stir puree back into soup. Season to taste with salt and pepper, and serve hot.

Note: The soup can be prepared up to 3 days in advance and refrigerated, tightly covered. Reheat it, covered, over low heat, stirring occasionally.

Variations:
* Substitute butternut squash for the acorn squash.
* Substitute molasses for the hoisin sauce, rum for the sherry, and cinnamon for the Chinese five-spice powder.

> Chinese five-spice powder is a spice mixture I use in place of cinnamon in dishes from many cultures. Cinnamon is one of the ingredients, along with anise, ginger, fennel, and pepper.

Potage Saint-Germain

When people think about a soup made with split peas they envision something very thick and hearty, like the Canadian Yellow Split Pea Soup with Sausage on page 51. This traditional French soup contains split peas and also garden peas and lettuce melded into the creamy base, so it's much lighter.

Makes 6 to 8 servings | Prep time: 15 minutes | Minimum cook time: 3 hours in a medium slow cooker

2 tablespoons unsalted butter

2 medium onions, chopped

1 carrot, chopped

2 celery ribs, chopped

7 cups Chicken Stock (page 21) or purchased stock

2 cups green split peas, rinsed

1 cup shredded romaine or iceberg lettuce

1 cup frozen peas, thawed

2 tablespoons chopped fresh parsley

2 tablespoons chopped fresh sage or 2 teaspoons dried

1 tablespoon fresh thyme or ½ teaspoon dried

1 bay leaf

1 cup half-and-half

Salt and freshly ground black pepper to taste

1. Heat butter in a medium skillet over medium-high heat. Add onion, carrot, and celery, and cook, stirring frequently, for 3 minutes, or until onion is translucent. Scrape mixture into the slow cooker.

2. Add stock, split peas, lettuce, peas, parsley, sage, thyme, and bay leaf to the slow cooker, and stir well. Cook on Low for 6 to 8 hours or on High for 3 to 4 hours, or until split peas have disintegrated.

3. If cooking on Low, raise the heat to High. Stir in half-and-half. Cook for an additional 30 to 40 minutes, or until soup is bubbly. Remove and discard bay leaf.

4. Allow soup to cool for 10 minutes. Either puree it with an immersion blender, or strain solids from soup and puree them in a food processor fitted with the steel blade or in a blender, and stir puree back into soup. Season to taste with salt and pepper, and serve hot.

Note: The soup can be prepared up to 3 days in advance and refrigerated, tightly covered. Reheat it, covered, over low heat, stirring occasionally.

Variation:

✳ Substitute yellow split peas for the green split peas, substitute yellow wax beans for the peas, and substitute tarragon for the sage.

> With almost all fresh herbs, the substitution with the dried form is 1 tablespoon fresh to 1 teaspoon dried. One exception to this, however, is thyme. The leaves are so small once dried that I've found that ½ teaspoon dried produces the same flavor as 1 tablespoon fresh.

Curried Parsnip Soup

Parsnips are one of the truly underutilized vegetables, and they are even sweeter and more delicate than their first cousin in the root vegetable camp, carrots. In this soup the roux is made with gluten-free rice flour, and the curry adds a bit of color with its flavor.

Makes 6 to 8 servings | Prep time: 20 minutes | Minimum cook time: 3 1/2 hours in a medium slow cooker

2 tablespoons unsalted butter

1 medium onion, diced

3 tablespoons white rice flour

1½ to 2 tablespoons curry powder, or to taste

6 parsnips, thinly sliced

1 apple, peeled, cored, and sliced

5 cups Chicken Stock (page 21) or purchased stock

½ cup heavy cream

Salt and freshly ground black pepper to taste

1. Melt butter in a medium saucepan over medium heat. Add onion, and cook, stirring frequently, for 3 minutes, or until onion is translucent. Reduce the heat to low, and stir in white rice flour and curry powder. Cook for 2 minutes, stirring constantly. Scrape mixture into the slow cooker.

2. Add parsnips, apple, and stock to the slow cooker, and stir well. Cook on Low for 6 to 8 hours or on High for 3 to 4 hours, or until carrots are tender.

3. If cooking on Low, raise the heat to High. Add cream and cook soup for an additional 10 to 20 minutes, or until simmering. Allow soup to cool for 10 minutes. Either puree it with an immersion blender, or strain solids from soup and puree them in a food processor fitted with the steel blade or in a blender, and stir puree back into soup. Season to taste with salt and pepper, and serve hot.

Note: The soup can be prepared up to 3 days in advance and refrigerated, tightly covered. Reheat it, covered, over low heat, stirring occasionally.

Variation:

∗ Substitute carrots for the parsnips.

While it's a good idea to toss out any dried herb or spice that's been opened for more than six months, abbreviate the life of curry powder to two months. This ground blend, which can contain up to 20 herbs and spices, loses its flavor and aroma very quickly.

Classic French Onion Soup

Deeply caramelized onions simmered for hours with hearty beef stock, red wine, and herbs is the quintessential bistro dish in my book. And there's no reason that people on gluten-free diets should not enjoy it, especially because there are now so many good gluten-free breads to turn into toast with gooey cheese.

Makes 6 to 8 servings | Active time: 20 minutes | Minimum cooking time: 8 1/2 hours in a medium slow cooker

4 tablespoons (½ stick) unsalted butter, cut into small pieces

¼ cup olive oil

3 pounds sweet onions, such as Vidalia or Bermuda, thinly sliced

1 tablespoon granulated sugar

Salt and freshly ground black pepper to taste

5 cups Beef Stock (page 23) or purchased stock

¾ cup dry red wine

3 tablespoons chopped fresh parsley

1 bay leaf

1 tablespoon fresh thyme or ½ teaspoon dried

6 slices gluten-free French or Italian bread, cut ½-inch thick

⅓ cup freshly grated Parmesan cheese

1 tablespoon cornstarch

1½ cups grated Gruyère or Swiss cheese

1. Set the slow cooker on High, and add butter and olive oil. Add onions once butter melts, and add sugar, salt, and pepper. Toss well to coat onions. Cook for 1 hour, remove the cover, and stir onions. Cook for an additional 3 to 4 hours, or until onions are golden brown.

2. Add beef stock, wine, parsley, bay leaf, and thyme to the slow cooker, and stir well. Cook on Low for 4 to 6 hours or on High for 2 to 3 hours, or until onions are very soft.

3. While soup cooks, preheat the oven to 450°F and cover a baking sheet with aluminum foil. Sprinkle bread with Parmesan cheese, and bake slices for 5 to 8 minutes, or until browned. Remove, and set aside.

4. Preheat the oven broiler. If cooking on Low, raise the heat to High. Mix cornstarch and 2 tablespoons cold water in a small cup. Stir mixture into the slow cooker, and cook for an additional 15 to 20 minutes, or until the liquid is bubbling and has slightly thickened. Remove and discard bay leaf, and season to taste with salt and pepper.

5. To serve, ladle hot soup into oven-proof soup bowls and top each with toast slice. Divide Gruyère on top of toast and broil 6 inches from heating element for 1 to 2 minutes, or until cheese melts and browns. Serve immediately.

Note: The soup can be prepared up to 3 days in advance and refrigerated, tightly covered. Reheat it, covered, over low heat, stirring occasionally.

If you don't have ovenproof soup bowls, you can still enjoy the gooey toast topping. Arrange the toast slices on a baking sheet lined with aluminum foil, and top with the cheese. Broil until the cheese melts, and then transfer the toasts to soup bowls with a wide spatula.

Chilled Garlicky Cream of Tomato Soup

This refreshing soup is like a cross between vichyssoise and cream of tomato; it contains potatoes that make it thick but also herbs, tomatoes, and garlic to enliven the flavor.

Makes 6 to 8 servings | Active time: 15 minutes | Minimum cook time: 2 1/4 hours in a medium slow cooker

2 tablespoons unsalted butter

1 medium onion, diced

4 garlic cloves, minced

4 cups Chicken Stock (page 21) or purchased stock

1½ pounds redskin potatoes, scrubbed and cut into ¾-inch cubes

1 (14.5-ounce) can diced tomatoes, undrained

2 tablespoons chopped fresh sage or 1 tablespoon dried

½ cup heavy cream

Salt and freshly ground black pepper to taste

½ cup sour cream (optional)

2 tablespoons snipped fresh chives

1. Heat butter in a small skillet over medium-high heat. Add onion and garlic, and cook, stirring frequently, for 3 minutes, or until onion is translucent. Scrape mixture into the slow cooker.

2. Add stock, potatoes, tomatoes, and sage to the slow cooker, and stir well. Cook on Low for 4½ to 6 hours or on High for 2 to 3 hours, or until potatoes are tender. Then, if cooking on Low, raise the heat to High. Add cream, and cook soup for an additional 10 to 20 minutes, or until simmering.

3. Allow soup to cool for 30 minutes. Either puree it with an immersion blender, or strain solids from soup and puree them in a food processor fitted with the steel blade or in a blender. Season to taste with salt and pepper, and chill thoroughly. To see, top soup with sour cream, if using, and sprinkle with chives.

Note: The soup can be prepared up to 3 days in advance and refrigerated, tightly covered. Stir it well before serving.

Variation:
* Substitute basil, oregano, or tarragon for the sage.

Cold foods, especially creamed soups, frequently need additional salt once chilled. The reason is that there are no vapors of steam that transmit aroma to the nose, which is a vital part of our eating experience with hot foods.

Vichyssoise with Poached Garlic

When whole cloves or garlic are poached or baked they become sweet and nutlike, and that's what happens in this delicious soup, which is served dotted with colorful green chives.

Makes 6 to 8 servings | Prep time: 20 minutes | Minimum cook time: 2¼ hours in a medium slow cooker

5 leeks, white part only

2 tablespoons unsalted butter

6 garlic cloves, peeled

2 large boiling potatoes (about 1½ pounds), peeled and cut into ¾-inch dice

4 cups Chicken Stock (page 21) or purchased stock

½ cup heavy whipping cream

Salt and freshly ground black pepper to taste

½ cup snipped fresh chives

1. Trim leeks, split lengthwise, and slice thinly. Place slices in a colander and rinse well under cold running water, rubbing with your fingers to dislodge all dirt. Shake leeks in the colander. Melt butter in a medium saucepan over medium heat. Add leeks and garlic cloves, and toss with butter. Cover the pan, reduce the heat to low, and cook for 10 minutes. Scrape mixture into the slow cooker.

2. Add potatoes and stock to the slow cooker, and stir well. Cook on Low for 4½ to 6 hours or on High for 2 to 3 hours, or until potatoes are tender. Then, if cooking on Low, raise the heat to High. Add cream, and cook soup for an additional 10 to 20 minutes, or until simmering.

3. Allow soup to cool for 30 minutes. Either puree it with an immersion blender, or strain solids from soup and puree them in a food processor fitted with the steel blade or in a blender. Season to taste with salt and pepper, and chill thoroughly. To serve, sprinkle each serving with chives.

Note: The soup can be prepared up to 3 days in advance and refrigerated, tightly covered. Stir well before serving.

Variations:

* Omit the garlic for a classic vichyssoise.
* Omit the cream, use a potato masher to mash about half of the potatoes, and serve the soup hot as a leek and potato soup.

Vichyssoise, actually an American invention despite the French name, is the Grandma of all cold summer soups. Chef Louis Diat created it during his tenure at The Ritz-Carlton Hotel in New York. Diat named the soup after Vichy, the resort town near his boyhood home in France.

Chilled Minted Pea Soup

This soup is drawn from English cuisine, and it's a really pretty light green color when served. While it's topped with a dollop of sour cream, the creaminess in the soup comes from the potatoes, which are blended with garden peas and herbs.

Makes 6 to 8 servings | Prep time: 20 minutes | Minimum cook time: 2 1/4 hours in a medium slow cooker

2 tablespoons unsalted butter

1 medium onion, peeled and chopped

4 cups Chicken Stock (page 21) or purchased stock

¾ pound boiling potatoes, peeled and cut into ¾-inch dice

2 (10-ounce) packages frozen peas, thawed

2 tablespoons chopped fresh parsley

2 tablespoons chopped fresh mint

¾ cup light cream

Salt and freshly ground black pepper to taste

½ to ¾ cup sour cream or crème fraîche

Shredded fresh mint for garnish

1. Heat butter in a small skillet over medium-high heat. Add onion, and cook, stirring frequently, for 3 minutes, or until onion is translucent. Scrape onion into the slow cooker.

2. Add stock, potatoes, peas, parsley, and mint to the slow cooker, and stir well. Cook on Low for 4 1/2 to 6 hours or on High for 2 to 3 hours, or until potatoes are tender. Then, if cooking on Low, raise the heat to High. Add cream, and cook soup for an additional 10 to 20 minutes, or until simmering.

3. Allow soup to cool for 30 minutes. Either puree it with an immersion blender, or strain solids from soup and puree them in a food processor fitted with the steel blade or in a blender. Season to taste with salt and pepper, and chill thoroughly. To serve, top each portion with a dollop of sour cream and some fresh mint.

Note: The soup can be prepared up to 3 days in advance and refrigerated, tightly covered. Stir well before serving.

Variation:

✳ Substitute ¼ cup chopped fresh tarragon for the mint.

Broadly speaking, potatoes are divided into "bakers," "boilers" and "all-purpose." "Boilers," such as redskin and Yukon Gold, have thin skins and hold their shape quite well when sliced. For this reason they are perfect for potato salad and for soups. "All-purpose" potatoes can be either baked or boiled and are generally white or red.

Manhattan Clam Chowder

This tomato-based version of chowder has as many devoted fans as the creamy version has in New England. The combination of the vegetables and herbs in the base make this recipe a real winner.

Makes 6 to 8 servings | Prep time: 15 minutes | Minimum cook time: 3 hours in a medium slow cooker

2 pints minced fresh clams

2 tablespoons olive oil

1 large onion, diced

2 garlic cloves, minced

2 celery ribs, diced

1 carrot, finely chopped

½ green bell pepper, seeds and ribs removed, and finely chopped

2 large redskin potatoes, scrubbed and cut into ¾-inch dice

1 (28-ounce) can crushed tomatoes, undrained

2 (8-ounce) bottles clam juice

3 tablespoons chopped fresh parsley

1 tablespoon fresh thyme or ½ teaspoon dried

2 teaspoons fresh oregano or ½ teaspoon dried

2 bay leaves

Salt and freshly ground black pepper to taste

1. Drain clams, reserving juice. Refrigerate clams until ready to use.

2. Heat oil in a medium skillet over medium heat. Add onion, garlic, celery, carrot, and green bell pepper. Cook, stirring frequently, for 3 minutes, or until onion is translucent. Scrape mixture into the slow cooker.

3. Add potatoes, tomatoes, clam juice, juice drained from clams, parsley, thyme, oregano, and bay leaves to the slow cooker, and stir well. Cook on Low for 5 to 7 hours or on High for 2½ to 3 hours, or until potatoes are almost tender.

4. If cooking on Low, raise the heat to High. Add clams, and continue to cook for an additional 20 to 40 minutes, or until clams are cooked through. Remove and discard bay leaves, season to taste with salt and pepper, and serve hot.

Note: The soup can be prepared up to 3 days in advance and refrigerated, tightly covered. Reheat it, covered, over low heat, stirring occasionally.

Variations:

* Substitute 1 pound of firm-fleshed white fish such as cod or halibut, cut into ⅓-inch dice, for the clams.
* Start by cooking 4 to 6 slices of bacon until crisp. Substitute 2 tablespoons of the bacon fat for the olive oil, and crumble the bacon into the soup when the clams are added.
* Add 1 (4-ounce) can chopped mild green chiles and 2 tablespoons chili powder to the slow cooker for Southwestern chowder.

It's now possible to find fresh minced clams in just about every supermarket. If they're not in the refrigerated case, check the freezer. If you must resort to canned clams, use 3 (6.5-ounce) cans for each pint of fresh clams specified.

New England Clam Chowder

Thickening soups with rice flour and cornstarch in the roux rather than all-purpose wheat flour is a trick you can transfer to all gluten-free cooking. It's perfect for this creamy chowder, the prototype for which I developed while catering on Nantucket many years ago.

Makes 6 to 8 servings | Prep time: 20 minutes | Minimum cook time: 3 hours in a medium slow cooker

2 pints fresh minced clams

3 tablespoons unsalted butter

1 large onion, diced

2 tablespoons white rice flour

1 tablespoon cornstarch

2 (8-ounce) bottles clam juice

2 celery ribs, sliced

2 large redskin potatoes, scrubbed and cut into ¾-inch dice

3 tablespoons chopped fresh parsley

1 tablespoon fresh thyme or ½ teaspoon dried

1 bay leaf

1 cup half-and-half

Salt and freshly ground black pepper to taste

1. Drain clams, reserving juice. Refrigerate clams until ready to use.

2. Heat butter in a small skillet over medium heat. Add onion, and cook, stirring frequently, for 3 minutes, or until onion is translucent. Reduce the heat to low, and stir in white rice flour and cornstarch. Cook for 2 minutes, stirring constantly. Raise the heat to medium high, and stir in 1 bottle clam juice. Bring to a boil, and simmer for 1 minute.

3. Pour mixture into the slow cooker. Add remaining bottled clam juice, juice drained from clams, celery, potatoes, parsley, thyme, and bay leaf to the slow cooker, and stir well. Cook on Low for 5 to 7 hours or on High for 2½ to 3 hours, or until potatoes are almost tender.

4. If cooking on Low, raise the heat to High. Stir in clams and half-and-half. Cook for an additional 20 to 40 minutes, or until clams are cooked through and soup is bubbly. Remove and discard bay leaf, season to taste with salt and pepper, and serve hot.

Note: The soup can be prepared up to 3 days in advance and refrigerated, tightly covered. Reheat it, covered, over low heat, stirring occasionally.

Variations:

* Omit the cream and add an additional bottle of clam juice for a lean Rhode Island–style clam chowder.

* Substitute 1 pound of firm-fleshed white fish such as cod or halibut, cut into ⅓-inch dice, for the clams.

> Dairy products such as cream and cheese tend to curdle if cooked in a slow cooker for the entire cooking time. Add them at the end and let them cook for no more than 1 hour, unless otherwise directed in the recipe.

Creamy Caribbean Seafood Chowder

Curry powder is a seasoning used in the Caribbean almost as much as in India. In this soup creamy coconut milk mellows the curry flavor, and vegetables make it visually appealing as well as delicious.

Makes 6 to 8 servings | Active time: 20 minutes | Minimum cook time: 3 1/2 hours in a medium slow cooker

2 tablespoons olive oil

1 medium onion, chopped

2 garlic cloves, minced

1 large carrot, diced

1 red bell pepper, seeds and ribs removed, and diced

1 small jalapeño or serrano chile, seeds and ribs removed, and finely chopped

1 tablespoon curry powder

1 tablespoon grated fresh ginger

½ teaspoon ground cinnamon

1 large sweet potato, peeled and cut into ¾-inch dice

3 cups Seafood Stock (page 25) or purchased stock

1 (14-ounce) can light coconut milk

¾ pound halibut or cod, or other firm-fleshed fish fillet, rinsed and cut into ¾-inch dice

Salt and freshly ground black pepper to taste

1. Heat oil in a large skillet over medium-high heat. Add onion, garlic, carrot, bell pepper, and chile, and cook, stirring frequently, for 3 minutes, or until onion is translucent. Reduce the heat to low, and stir in curry powder, ginger, and cinnamon. Cook for 1 minute, stirring constantly. Scrape mixture into the slow cooker.

2. Add sweet potato, stock, and coconut milk to the slow cooker, and stir well. Cook soup on Low for 4 to 6 hours or High for 2 to 3 hours, or until vegetables are almost tender. Remove ¼ of solids from soup with a slotted spoon, and place them in a food processor fitted with a steel blade or in a blender. Puree until smooth, and stir puree back into soup.

3. If cooking on Low, raise the heat to High. Cook for an additional 40 to 50 minutes, or until fish is cooked through and flakes easily. Season to taste with salt and pepper, and serve hot.

Note: The soup can be prepared up to 3 days in advance and refrigerated, tightly covered. Reheat it, covered, over low heat, stirring occasionally.

Variations:

❊ Substitute chicken stock for the seafood stock and substitute ¾ pound boneless, skinless chicken breast, cut into ½-inch dice, for the fish. Add the chicken at the onset of the cooking time.

❊ Substitute vegetable stock for the seafood stock, and substitute ¾-pound extra-firm tofu for the fish.

Many a cook has suffered a scraped·knuckle while grating fresh ginger. If the ginger knob is large, peel only the amount you think you'll need and hold on to the remainder. If you're down to a small part, impale it on a fork and use that as your grating handle.

Potato Soup with Bacon and Cheddar

I've never met a potato I didn't like, and that holds true for soups too. The bacon adds a smoky nuance to the rich flavor. This soup is one of my favorite ways to begin a fall or winter dinner.

Makes 6 to 8 servings | Active time: 20 minutes | Minimum cook time: 4 hours in a medium slow cooker

¼ pound bacon, cut into 1-inch lengths

1 medium onion, diced

1 carrot, diced

1 celery rib, trimmed and diced

1 garlic clove, minced

2 pounds redskin potatoes, scrubbed and cut into ¾-inch dice

4 cups Chicken Stock (page 21) or purchased stock

2 teaspoons fresh thyme or ½ teaspoon dried

2 cups grated sharp cheddar cheese

1 cup half-and-half

Salt and freshly ground black pepper to taste

1. Cook bacon in a heavy skillet over medium-high heat until crisp. Remove bacon from the pan with a slotted spoon, drain on paper towels, and set aside. Discard all but 3 tablespoons bacon grease from the skillet.

2. Add onion, carrot, celery, and garlic to the skillet, and cook, stirring frequently, for 3 minutes, or until onion is translucent. Scrape mixture into the slow cooker.

3. Add potatoes, stock, and thyme to the slow cooker, and stir well. Cook on Low for 6 to 8 hours or on High for 3 to 4 hours, or until vegetables are tender.

4. If cooking on Low, raise the heat to High. Mash some of vegetables with a potato masher until desired consistency; the more that is mashed the thicker the soup will be. Add 1½ cups cheese and half-and-half, and cook for 20 to 30 minutes, or until cheese melts and soup simmers. Season to taste with salt and pepper, and serve hot, sprinkling each serving with crumbled bacon and remaining cheese.

Note: The soup can be prepared up to 3 days in advance and refrigerated, tightly covered. Reheat it, covered, over low heat, stirring occasionally.

Variations:

✳ Substitute Swiss cheese for the cheddar cheese, and add 1 (10-ounce) package frozen chopped spinach, thawed and drained well, along with the cream and cheese.

✳ Substitute oregano for the thyme, and add 1 (4-ounce) can chopped mild green chiles, drained, and 3 tablespoons chopped fresh cilantro to the soup.

✳ Substitute pancetta for the bacon, and substitute 1 cup crumbled Gorgonzola and ½ cup shredded fontina for the cheddar.

> If you're having problems separating strips of bacon, throw the whole amount into a pan as though it were a single slice. Within a few moments, the bacon will have softened enough to make it easy to separate individual slices.

Canadian Yellow Split Pea Soup with Sausage

Yellow split peas taste identical to their drab green cousins, but I think that they make a far prettier soup. Using sausage instead of ham also adds more complex flavors to this comfort food classic.

Makes 6 to 8 servings | Prep time: 15 minutes | Minimum cook time: 3 hours in a medium slow cooker

⅓ pound bulk pork sausage

1 large onion, finely chopped

1 celery rib, finely chopped

1 carrot, finely chopped

2 garlic cloves, minced

1 pound yellow split peas, rinsed

6 cups Ham Stock (page 21), Chicken Stock (page 21), or purchased stock

2 tablespoons chopped fresh parsley

1 tablespoon fresh thyme or ½ teaspoon dried

1 bay leaf

Salt and freshly ground black pepper to taste

1. Heat oil in a medium skillet over medium-high heat. Crumble sausage into the skillet, breaking up lumps with a fork. Cook sausage for 3 to 5 minutes, or until browned. Remove sausage from the skillet with a slotted spoon, and transfer it to the slow cooker. Discard all but 2 tablespoons sausage grease from the skillet.

2. Add onion, celery, carrot, and garlic to the skillet. Cook, stirring frequently, for 3 minutes, or until onion is translucent. Scrape mixture into the slow cooker.

3. Add split peas, stock, parsley, thyme, and bay leaf to the slow cooker, and stir well. Cook on Low for 6 to 8 hours or on High for 3 to 4 hours, or until split peas have disintegrated. Remove and discard bay leaf, season to taste with salt and pepper, and serve hot.

Note: The soup can be prepared up to 3 days in advance and refrigerated, tightly covered. Reheat it, covered, over low heat, stirring occasionally.

Variations:

* Substitute green split peas for the yellow split peas.
* Substitute ½ pound smoked ham steak, cut into ½-inch cubes, for the sausage. No browning is necessary.
* Substitute vegetable stock for the meat-based stocks, omit the ham, increase the thyme to 1½ tablespoons, and add 1 tablespoon chopped fresh sage.

We know that pea soup has been around for many centuries; Aristophanes mentioned it in his play *The Birds*. Back in the sixth century BCE pea soup was the food sold by the street vendors in Athens.

Cháo (Vietnamese Rice Chowder with Pork)

This thick soup is a Vietnamese version of congee, which is served for breakfast as well as at other times of the day in much of Southeast Asia. The ginger, cilantro, and fried shallots create a subtle soup with hearty flavor.

Makes 6 to 8 servings | *Active time: 20 minutes* | *Minimum cook time: 3³/₄ hours in a medium slow cooker*

2 thick or 3 thin scallions, trimmed

¾ cup short-grain (sushi) rice

¼ pound ground pork

1 tablespoon fish sauce *(nam pla)*

½ teaspoon granulated sugar

1 tablespoon vegetable oil, divided

1 shallot, minced

6 cups Chicken Stock (page 21) or purchased stock

3 tablespoons very fine julienne of fresh ginger

Salt and freshly ground white pepper to taste

1 to 2 tablespoons chopped fresh cilantro

Salt and freshly ground white pepper to taste

1. Thinly slice white parts of the scallions. Slice 4 inches of the green tops into ¼-inch slices. Set aside white rings and green tops separately. Rinse rice in a sieve until the water is clear.

2. Combine pork with fish sauce and sugar. Heat ½ of oil in a small skillet over medium-high heat. Crumble pork into the skillet, breaking up lumps with a fork, and cook until browned. Scrape pork into the slow cooker. Heat remaining oil in the skillet, and add shallot. Cook for 3 to 5 minutes, or until browned. Scrape shallot into the slow cooker.

3. Add stock, rice, white scallion rings, and ginger to the slow cooker, and stir well. Cook on High for 3 to 3½ hours, or until rice is very soft. Season to taste with salt and pepper, and serve hot, sprinkling each serving with cilantro and scallion tops.

Note: The soup can be prepared up to 3 days in advance and refrigerated, tightly covered. Reheat it, covered, over low heat, stirring occasionally.

Variations:

✷ Substitute ground turkey or ground chicken for the pork.

✷ Substitute seafood stock for the chicken stock, and substitute ½ pint minced clams for the pork. The clams do not need any pretreatment; add the fish sauce to the slow cooker.

Fish sauce, a salty sauce with an extremely pungent odor, is made from fermented fish, primarily anchovies. It's used as a dipping sauce/condiment and seasoning ingredient throughout Southeast Asia. *Nam pla* is the Thai term; it's known as *nuoc nam* in Vietnam and *shottsuru* in Japan. Soy sauce is a good substitution, although fish sauce is now easy to find in most supermarkets.

Szechwan Hot and Sour Soup

Back in the 1960s, when the fiery flavors of Szechwan cuisine first arrived in this country, I became addicted to this soup and have worked for years to create the ultimate version. I hope you agree with me that this is it.

Makes 6 to 8 servings | *Active time: 20 minutes* | *Minimum cook time: 3³/₄ hours in a medium slow cooker*

12 large dried shiitake mushrooms

1 cup boiling water

½ pound boneless pork loin

5 cups Chicken Stock (page 21) or purchased stock

½ pound firm tofu, well drained and cut into ¾-inch dice

⅓ cup rice wine vinegar

2 tablespoons soy sauce

1 tablespoon Asian sesame oil

½ teaspoon freshly ground black pepper, or to taste

2 tablespoons cornstarch

2 large eggs, lightly beaten

4 scallions, white parts and 4 inches of green tops, trimmed and thinly sliced

1. Soak shiitake mushrooms in water for 10 minutes, pressing mushrooms down with the back of a spoon to keep them submerged. Cut all fat from pork, and cut into thin slices. Stack slices, and cut into thin ribbons. Place pork in the slow cooker.

2. Remove mushrooms from the cup, and strain soaking liquid through a coffee filter or paper towel into the slow cooker. Discard stems, and slice mushrooms into thin slices. Add mushrooms to the slow cooker along with stock, tofu, vinegar, soy sauce, sesame oil, and pepper, and stir well.

3. Cook on Low for 5 to 7 hours or on High for 2½ to 3½ hours, or until pork is cooked through.

4. If cooking on Low, raise the heat to High. Combine cornstarch and 2 tablespoons cold water in a small cup. Stir cornstarch mixture into soup. Cook on High for 15 to 20 minutes, or until the liquid has thickened and is bubbly. Stir eggs into soup, and continue to stir so eggs form thin strands. Cover the slow cooker, and bring soup back to a simmer. Season to taste with salt and pepper, and serve hot, sprinkling each serving with scallion slices.

Note: The soup can be prepared up to 3 days in advance and refrigerated, tightly covered. Reheat it, covered, over low heat, stirring occasionally.

Variations:

❋ Substitute vegetable stock for the chicken stock, omit the pork, and increase the tofu to 1 pound.

❋ Substitute seafood stock for the chicken stock and substitute cooked shrimp for the pork. Add the shrimp 30 minutes before the soup will be cooked to warm them.

❋ Substitute boneless, skinless chicken breast, chicken thigh, or duck breast for the pork.

Fresh shiitake mushrooms may be a relative newcomer to the American produce section, but they are the granddaddy of all cultivated mushrooms. The Japanese have been cultivating them for more than 2,000 years. The ancient Greeks and Romans did not cultivate mushrooms, contrary to popular belief; they merely encouraged wild ones to grow. It was not until the eighteenth century, when Olivier de Serres was agronomist to French King Louis XIV, that mushroom cultivation began in Europe.

Chapter 3

Satisfying Soups as Supper

There's a fine line between what I consider a soup hearty enough to make it the centerpiece of a meal and a stew. My definition is that a soup can be eaten only with a spoon because everything that is in it is small enough to fit on the spoon, and that it's in a bowl because there's too much liquid to be feasibly served on a plate.

Unlike the soups in Chapter 2, these are a meal in and of themselves. I usually serve a tossed salad to start because there's little to crunch in a soup meal. I've noted what grain goes well with each soup in the individual listing if one is needed. Sometimes there are potatoes in the soup so the carb quotient is accounted for.

Classic Cuban Black Bean Soup

This soup is so thick and hearty that devoted carnivores can't get enough of it. Serve it over some brown rice, and you've got a complete protein too. For a side salad I tend to do a pico de gallo or jicama salad to continue the Hispanic theme.

Makes 4 to 6 servings | Prep time: 15 minutes | Minimum cook time: 4 hours in a medium slow cooker

1 pound dried black beans

¼ cup olive oil

1 large onion, diced

1 green bell pepper, seeds and ribs removed, and finely chopped

6 garlic cloves, minced

1 or 2 jalapeño or serrano chiles, seeds removed, and finely chopped

1 tablespoon ground cumin

2 teaspoons ground coriander

5 cups Vegetable Stock (page 24) or purchased stock

Salt to taste

Freshly ground black pepper to taste

¼ cup chopped fresh cilantro

Freshly ground black pepper to taste

FOR SERVING:

Sour cream

Lime wedges

Sweet potato chips

1. Rinse beans in a colander and place them in a mixing bowl covered with cold water. Allow beans to soak for at least 6 hours, or overnight. Or place beans into a saucepan and bring to a boil over high heat. Boil 1 minute. Turn off the heat, cover the pan, and soak beans for 1 hour. With either soaking method, drain beans, discard soaking water, and begin cooking as soon as possible.

2. Heat oil in a medium skillet over medium heat. Add onion, green bell pepper, garlic, and chile. Cook, stirring frequently, for 3 minutes, or until onion is translucent. Reduce the heat to low, and stir in cumin and coriander. Cook for 1 minute, stirring constantly. Scrape the mixture into the slow cooker.

3. Place drained beans in the slow cooker, and stir in stock. Cook soup on Low for 8 to 10 hours or High for 4 to 5 hours, or until beans are soft. Add salt during the last hour of cooking.

4. Allow soup to cool for 10 minutes. Either puree it with an immersion blender, or strain solids from soup and puree them in a food processor fitted with the steel blade or in a blender, and stir puree back into soup. Stir in cilantro, season to taste with salt and pepper, and serve hot. Top with sweet potato chips and a dollop of sour cream and pass lime wedges.

Note: The soup can be prepared up to 3 days in advance and refrigerated, tightly covered. Reheat it, covered, over low heat, stirring occasionally.

Variation:

❋ If you don't care if this soup is vegetarian, add ¾ pound browned chorizo to it, and substitute ham stock or chicken stock for the vegetable stock.

You can rinse bunches of parsley, cilantro, and dill, trim off the stems, and then wrap small bundles and freeze them. When you need some, you can "chop" it with the blunt side of a knife. It will chop easily when frozen, and this method produces far better flavor than dried.

Spanish Fish Soup with Potatoes, Greens, and Aïoli (Caldo de Perro)

Every cuisine that borders a body of water has a wonderful selection of fish stews that were created by the fishermen with whatever they caught in the nets that day. This one from the region around Barcelona features colorful escarole and potatoes, and it's topped with a garlicky mayonnaise sauce.

Makes 4 to 6 servings | *Prep time: 20 minutes* | *Minimum cook time: 3 1/2 hours in a medium slow cooker*

1½ pounds halibut, cod, monkfish, snapper, sea bass, or any firm-fleshed white fish

2 tablespoons olive oil

2 medium onions, diced

7 garlic cloves, minced, divided

4 cups Seafood Stock (page 25) or purchased stock

½ cup dry white wine

2 tablespoons freshly squeezed lemon juice

1 pound redskin potatoes, scrubbed and cut into ½-inch dice

2 tablespoons chopped fresh parsley

1 tablespoon fresh thyme or ½ teaspoon dried

1 bay leaf

½ pound escarole

Salt and freshly ground black pepper to taste

½ cup mayonnaise

1 teaspoon grated lemon zest

1. Rinse fish and pat dry with paper towels. Remove and discard any skin or bones. Cut fish into 1-inch cubes. Refrigerate fish until ready to use, covered with plastic wrap.

2. Heat oil in a small skillet over medium-high heat. Add onion and 3 garlic cloves, and cook, stirring frequently, for 3 minutes, or until onion is translucent. Scrape the mixture into the slow cooker.

3. Add stock, wine, lemon juice, potatoes, parsley, thyme, and bay leaf to the slow cooker, and stir well. Cook on Low for 6 to 8 hours or on High for 3 to 4 hours, or until potatoes are tender.

4. While soup cooks, prepare escarole. Rinse leaves, and discard stems. Cut leaves crosswise into ½-inch slices. Make sauce by combining mayonnaise, lemon zest, and remaining garlic. Refrigerate until ready to serve.

5. If cooking on Low, raise the heat to High. Add fish and escarole. Cook for 40 to 55 minutes, or until fish is just cooked through and flakes easily. Remove and discard bay leaf, season to taste with salt and pepper, and serve hot. Pass sauce separately.

Note: The soup can be prepared up to 3 days in advance and refrigerated, tightly covered. Reheat it, covered, over low heat, stirring occasionally.

Variations:

* Substitute Swiss chard or collard greens for the escarole.
* Substitute boneless, skinless chicken for the fish, and substitute chicken stock for the fish stock. Add the chicken to the slow cooker at the onset of the cooking time.

Basque Bean and Cabbage Soup (*Garbure*)

This hearty soup reflects the earthiness of traditional Basque cooking. The use of smoked paprika adds a blushing color to it as well as a smoky nuance.

Makes 4 to 6 servings | *Active time: 20 minutes* | *Minimum cook time: 4 hours in a medium slow cooker*

1½ cups dried white navy beans

2 tablespoons olive oil

1 medium onion, chopped

3 garlic cloves, minced

1 carrot, chopped

1 celery rib, chopped

3 tablespoons smoked Spanish paprika

6 cups Vegetable Stock (page 24)
or purchased stock

¼ cup chopped fresh parsley

1 tablespoon fresh thyme
or ½ teaspoon dried

1 bay leaf

1 pound redskin potatoes, scrubbed and
cut into ¾-inch dice

6 cups firmly packed thinly sliced
green cabbage

Salt and freshly ground black pepper
to taste

1. Rinse beans in a colander and place them in a mixing bowl covered with cold water. Allow beans to soak for at least 6 hours, or overnight. Or place beans into a saucepan and bring to a boil over high heat. Boil 1 minute. Turn off the heat, cover the pan, and soak beans for 1 hour. With either soaking method, drain beans, discard soaking water, and begin cooking as soon as possible.

2. Heat oil in a skillet over medium-high heat. Add onion, garlic, carrot, and celery. Cook, stirring frequently, for 3 minutes, or until onion is translucent. Reduce the heat to low, and stir in paprika. Cook for 1 minute, stirring constantly. Scrape mixture into the slow cooker.

3. Place drained beans in the slow cooker, and stir in stock, parsley, thyme, bay leaf, potatoes, and cabbage. Cook soup on Low for 8 to 10 hours or High for 4 to 5 hours, or until beans are soft. Add salt during the last hour of cooking.

4. Remove and discard bay leaf, season to taste with salt and pepper, and serve hot.

Note: The soup can be prepared up to 3 days in advance and refrigerated, tightly covered. Reheat it, covered, over low heat, stirring occasionally.

Variation:

✳ For a more Italian flavor, omit the smoked paprika, and add 2 tablespoons chopped fresh basil (or 2 teaspoons dried) and 2 tablespoons chopped fresh oregano (or 2 teaspoons dried).

> When cooking bulky foods such as cabbage, chances are good that all the cabbage will not be covered with broth at the beginning of the cooking process. About midway through, push it down because by then it will have wilted considerably.

Minestrone with Herb Oil

The expansion of gluten-free shelf-stable products during the past few years has been exciting to anyone following the diet, and one of the biggest pleasures is pasta made from brown rice. If you can't find small shells, you can break apart long strands of linguine or fettuccine for this hearty vegetarian soup. The herb oil adds a fresh aroma and flavor to the long-simmered soup.

Makes 4 to 6 servings | Active time: 25 minutes | Minimum cook time: 3 hours in a medium slow cooker

SOUP

3 tablespoons olive oil

1 large onion, diced

2 garlic cloves, minced

1 large carrot, sliced

½ fennel bulb, cored and diced

2 cups firmly packed thinly sliced green cabbage

5 cups Vegetable Stock (page 24) or purchased stock

1 (14.5-ounce) can diced tomatoes, undrained

2 tablespoons tomato paste

2 tablespoons chopped fresh parsley

1 tablespoon chopped fresh oregano or 1 teaspoon dried

1 tablespoon fresh thyme or ½ teaspoon dried

1 bay leaf

1 medium zucchini, diced

1 medium yellow squash, diced

1 (15-ounce) can garbanzo beans, drained and rinsed

½ cup freshly grated Parmesan cheese

¼ pound gluten-free small pasta such as shells, cooked according to package directions until al dente

Salt and freshly ground black pepper to taste

HERB OIL

¾ cup firmly packed parsley leaves

2 garlic cloves, minced

2 tablespoons chopped fresh basil or 2 teaspoons dried

1 tablespoon chopped fresh rosemary or 1 teaspoon dried

½ cup olive oil

Salt and freshly ground black pepper to taste

1. Heat oil in a large skillet over medium-high heat. Add onion, garlic, carrot, fennel, and cabbage. Cook, stirring frequently, for 3 minutes, or until onion is translucent. Scrape mixture into the slow cooker.

2. Add stock, tomatoes, tomato paste, parsley, oregano, thyme, bay leaf, zucchini, and yellow squash to the slow cooker, and stir well. Cook on Low for 6 to 8 hours or on High for 3 to 4 hours, or until vegetables are almost tender.

3. If cooking on Low, raise the heat to High. Add beans and Parmesan to the slow cooker, and cook for 20 to 30 minutes, or until simmering. Remove and discard bay leaf, add pasta, and season to taste with salt and pepper.

4. While soup simmers, prepare herb oil. Combine parsley, garlic, basil, rosemary, and oil in a food processor fitted with the steel blade or in a blender. Puree until smooth. Season to taste with salt and pepper, and scrape mixture into a bowl.

5. To serve, ladle soup into bowls, and pass herb oil separately.

Note: The soup can be prepared up to 3 days in advance and refrigerated, tightly covered. Reheat it, covered, over low heat, stirring occasionally.

Variation:

∗ Substitute chicken stock for the vegetable stock, and add ½ pound boneless, skinless chicken, cut into ¾-inch cubes, at the onset of the cooking time.

New England Seafood Stew

This is a heartier fish soup than most because it contains both smoky bacon and spicy linguiça sausage. I also love the nuances of orange in the broth, and with potatoes included it's truly a meal.

Makes 4 to 6 servings | Prep time: 20 minutes | Minimum cook time: 3 1/2 hours in a medium slow cooker

½ pound thick cod fillet

½ pound swordfish fillet

½ pound bay scallops

2 juice oranges, washed

¼ pound bacon, cut into 1-inch pieces

1 medium onion, diced

1 carrot, sliced

1 celery rib, sliced

3 garlic cloves, minced

½ pound linguiça sausage, diced

1 (14.5-ounce) can diced tomatoes, undrained

½ cup dry red wine

3 cups Seafood Stock (page 25) or purchased stock

3 tablespoons chopped fresh basil or 1 teaspoon dried

2 tablespoons chopped fresh parsley

1 tablespoon fresh thyme or ½ teaspoon dried

1 bay leaf

2 large redskin potatoes, scrubbed and cut into ¾-inch dice

Salt and freshly ground black pepper to taste

1. Rinse fish and pat dry with paper towels. Remove and discard any skin or bones. Cut fish into 1-inch cubes. Refrigerate fish and scallops until ready to use, covered with plastic wrap. Grate off orange zest, and then squeeze oranges for juice. Set aside.

2. Cook bacon in a heavy skillet over medium-high heat for 5 to 7 minutes, or until crisp. Remove bacon from the pan with a slotted spoon, and transfer it to the slow cooker. Discard all but 2 tablespoons of bacon grease.

3. Add onion, carrot, celery, and garlic to the skillet. Cook, stirring frequently, for 3 minutes, or until onion is translucent. Add linguiça, and cook for 2 minutes more. Scrape mixture into the slow cooker.

4. Add tomatoes, orange zest, orange juice, red wine, stock, basil, parsley, thyme, bay leaf, and potatoes to the slow cooker, and stir well. Cook on Low for 6 to 8 hours or on High for 3 to 4 hours, or until vegetables are soft.

5. If cooking on Low, raise the heat to High. Add fish, and cook for 30 to 50 minutes, or until fish is cooked through and flakes easily. Remove and discard bay leaf, season to taste with salt and pepper, and serve hot.

Note: The soup can be prepared up to 3 days in advance and refrigerated, tightly covered. Reheat it, covered, over low heat, stirring occasionally.

Variation:

✳ Substitute boneless, skinless chicken for the fish and substitute chicken stock for the fish stock. Add the chicken to the slow cooker at the onset of the cooking time.

There's a Portuguese influence on the cooking of the pocket of New England that was active during the whaling trade in the nineteenth century, including the region from Nantucket and Cape Cod to New Bedford and Fall River. That's why it is common to find linguiça sausage in recipes from Eastern Massachusetts.

Indian Curried Beef Soup

This is a heartier variation on Mulligatawny, which is traditionally made with chicken, and the soup dates from the British era in India. The soup is thickened by the puree of the vegetables and nuts in a broth made with coconut milk as well as spices.

Makes 4 to 6 servings | Prep time: 25 minutes | Minimum cook time: 3 1/2 hours in a medium slow cooker

1 (1¼ to 1½-pound) boneless chuck roast

2 tablespoons vegetable oil

1 large onion, diced

3 garlic cloves, minced

2 tablespoons curry powder or to taste

1 teaspoon ground cumin

1 teaspoon turmeric

4 cups Beef Stock (page 23) or purchased stock

2 large redskin potatoes, cut into ¾-inch dice

1 carrot, diced

1 cup blanched almonds

1 cup canned unsweetened coconut milk

2 tablespoons freshly squeezed lime juice

3 tablespoons chopped fresh cilantro

Salt and freshly ground black pepper to taste

1. Preheat the oven broiler, and line a broiler pan with heavy-duty aluminum foil. Broil beef for 3 minutes per side, or until browned. Transfer beef to the slow cooker, and pour in any juices that have collected in the pan.

2. Heat vegetable oil in a medium skillet over medium heat. Add onion and garlic, and cook, stirring frequently, for 3 minutes, or until onion is translucent. Reduce the heat to low, and stir in curry powder, cumin, and turmeric. Cook over low heat for 1 minute, stirring constantly. Scrape mixture into the slow cooker.

3. Add stock, potatoes, carrot, and almonds to the slow cooker, and stir well. Cook on Low for 8 to 10 hours or on High for 4 to 5 hours, or until beef is tender. Remove beef from the slow cooker with tongs, and set aside. Cut beef into 1-inch cubes, and keep warm.

4. Allow soup to cool for 10 minutes. Either puree it with an immersion blender, or strain solids from soup and puree them in a food processor fitted with the steel blade or in a blender, and stir puree back into soup.

5. If cooking on Low, raise the heat to High. Stir in coconut milk, lime juice, and cilantro, and return beef to the slow cooker. Cook soup for an additional 30 to 45 minutes, or until simmering. Season to taste with salt and pepper, and serve hot.

Note: The soup can be prepared up to 3 days in advance and refrigerated, tightly covered. Reheat it, covered, over low heat, stirring occasionally.

Variation:
* Substitute boneless skinless chicken thighs for the beef; they do not need to be browned. Substitute chicken stock for the beef stock.

> Nuts are a great way to thicken dishes when following a gluten-free diet. The nuts add a nuance of flavor, but the majority of the nut becomes pulp which then thickens liquid in the same way as wheat flour.

Mexican Chicken Tortilla Soup

All corn is naturally gluten-free, and strips of crispy corn tortillas are a wonderful topping for this authentically Mexican soup served topped with avocado and cheese.

Makes 4 to 6 servings | Prep time: 25 minutes | Minimum cook time: 3 hours in a medium slow cooker

1 pound boneless, skinless chicken meat (breasts or thighs)

2 tablespoons olive oil

2 medium onions, diced

4 garlic cloves, minced

2 tablespoons chopped fresh oregano or 2 teaspoons dried

2 teaspoon ground cumin

1 (14.5-ounce) can diced tomatoes, undrained

5 cups Chicken Stock (page 21) or purchased stock

2 tablespoons tomato paste

1 celery rib, sliced

1 small zucchini, trimmed and cut into ¾-inch dice

1 carrot, sliced

1 medium redskin potato, scrubbed and cut into ½-inch dice

Salt and freshly ground black pepper to taste

½ cup vegetable oil

4 corn tortillas, cut into ½-inch strips

1 ripe avocado, peeled and diced

⅔ cup grated Monterey Jack cheese

½ cup chopped fresh cilantro

1. Rinse chicken and pat dry with paper towels. Trim chicken of all visible fat, and cut into ¾-inch cubes. Place chicken in the slow cooker.

2. Heat olive oil in a large skillet over medium-high heat. Add onions and garlic, and cook, stirring frequently, for 3 minutes, or until onions are translucent. Reduce the heat to low, and stir in oregano and cumin. Cook for 1 minute, stirring constantly. Add tomatoes and stir well. Puree mixture in a food processor fitted with a steel blade or in a blender. Scrape puree into the slow cooker, and add stock and tomato paste. Stir well.

3. Add chicken, celery, zucchini, carrot, and potato to the slow cooker, and stir well. Cook on Low for 6 to 8 hours or on High for 3 to 4 hours, or until chicken is cooked through and no longer pink and potatoes are tender. Season to taste with salt and pepper.

4. About 30 minutes before soup will be finished, heat vegetable oil in a medium skillet over high heat. Add tortilla strips, and fry until crisp. Remove strips from the pan with a slotted spoon, and drain on paper towels.

5. To serve, ladle hot soup into bowls, and garnish each serving with fried tortilla strips, avocado, cheese, and cilantro.

Note: The soup can be prepared up to 3 days in advance and refrigerated, tightly covered. Reheat it, covered, over low heat, stirring occasionally.

Variation:

✳ Substitute vegetable stock for the chicken stock, and substitute extra-firm tofu for the chicken.

To determine if an avocado is ready to eat, insert a wooden toothpick into the stem end; if it can be inserted with ease, the avocado is ready. After cutting the avocado apart, if you discover that it is not yet ripe, coat the exposed surfaces with margarine or butter and allow it to continue ripening at room temperature.

Southwest Creamy Chicken, Corn, and Sweet Potato Chowder

Chipotle chiles are smoked jalapeño chiles that add that smoky nuance to the creamy chowder thickened with cornmeal that is flecked with corn and other vegetables. Some warm corn tortillas and a salad with avocado work well to complete the meal.

Makes 4 to 6 servings | *Active time: 20 minutes* | *Minimum cook time: 3 $\frac{1}{2}$ hours in a medium slow cooker*

1 pound boneless, skinless chicken meat (breasts or thighs)

3 tablespoons unsalted butter

1 red or orange bell pepper, seeds and ribs removed, and chopped

1 large onion, diced

2 garlic cloves, minced

2 large sweet potatoes, peeled and cut into ¾-inch dice

4 cups Chicken Stock (page 21) or purchased stock

2 canned chipotle chiles in adobo sauce, finely chopped

2 tablespoons yellow cornmeal

1 (15-ounce) can creamed corn

1 cup fresh corn kernels or frozen corn, thawed

1½ cups light cream

Salt and freshly ground black pepper to taste

¼ cup firmly packed fresh cilantro leaves

1. Rinse chicken and pat dry with paper towels. Trim chicken of all visible fat, and cut into ¾-inch cubes. Place chicken in the slow cooker.

2. Heat butter in a skillet over medium-high heat. Add bell pepper, onion, and garlic. Cook, stirring frequently, for 3 minutes, or until onion is translucent. Scrape mixture into the slow cooker.

3. Add sweet potatoes, stock, chipotle chiles, and cornmeal to the slow cooker, and stir well. Cook on Low for 6 to 8 hours or on High for 3 to 4 hours, or until potatoes are almost tender.

4. If cooking on Low, raise the heat to High. Stir in creamed corn, corn, and cream. Cook for an additional 30 to 40 minutes, or until corn is cooked and soup is bubbly. Season to taste with salt and pepper, and serve hot, sprinkling each serving with cilantro.

Note: The soup can be prepared up to 3 days in advance and refrigerated, tightly covered. Reheat it, covered, over low heat, stirring occasionally.

Variation:

* Substitute 1 (4-ounce) can chopped mild green chiles for the chipotle peppers for a milder soup.

There is evidence to support the idea that chicken stock really does contain medicinal qualities; perhaps your grandma was right all along. In 1993, University of Nebraska Medical Center researcher Dr. Stephen Rennard published a study stating that chicken soup contains an anti-inflammatory mechanism that eases the symptoms of upper respiratory tract infections. Other studies also showed that the chicken soup was equally medicinal if made without vegetables; it was the chicken itself.

Beet and Cabbage Borscht with Beef

The pigment that gives beets their rich, purple-crimson color—betacyanin—is also a powerful cancer-fighting agent. Beets' potential effectiveness against colon cancer, in particular, has been demonstrated in several studies. So that's additional reason to enjoy this hearty winter soup.

Makes 4 to 6 servings | Prep time: 20 minutes | Minimum cook time: 4 hours in a medium slow cooker

1 (1¼ to 1½-pound) beef brisket

2 large boiling potatoes, peeled and cut into 1-inch cubes

1½ pounds beets, peeled and cut into 1-inch cubes

1 large onion, cut into 1-inch cubes

4 cups Beef Stock (page 23) or purchased stock

2 cups firmly packed shredded green cabbage (about ¼ small head)

2 tablespoons granulated sugar

1 tablespoon freshly squeezed lemon juice

Salt and freshly ground black pepper to taste

Sour cream, optional

1. Preheat the oven broiler, and line a broiler pan with heavy-duty aluminum foil. Broil beef for 3 minutes per side, or until browned. Transfer beef to the slow cooker, and pour in any juices that have collected in the pan.

2. Place potatoes, beets, and onion in the work bowl of a food processor fitted with a steel blade. Chop finely using the on-and-off pulsing action or chop by hand. Scrape mixture into the slow cooker.

3. Add stock, cabbage, sugar, and lemon juice into the slow cooker, and stir well. Cook on Low for 8 to 10 hours or on High for 4 to 5 hours, or until beef is tender.

4. Remove beef from the slow cooker with tongs, and cut across the grain into thin slices. Set aside. Remove ⅓ of vegetables from the slow cooker with a slotted spoon. Puree vegetables in a food processor fitted with a steel blade or in a blender until smooth. Return puree to soup, and stir well. Season to taste with salt and pepper, and serve hot, placing slices of beef in each bowl. Pass sour cream separately, if using.

Note: The soup can be prepared up to 3 days in advance and refrigerated, tightly covered. Reheat it, covered, over low heat, stirring occasionally.

Variation:
* Substitute chicken stock for the beef stock, and substitute boneless, skinless chicken meat, cut into ¾-inch cubes, for the beef. The cooking time can be reduced by 2 hours on Low or 1 hour on High.

> Borscht, always made with beets and sometimes made with meat, is of Russian and Polish origin. It was popular with the Jews who emigrated from those countries in the late nineteenth century, and by the 1930s, resorts in New York's Catskill Mountains that featured Jewish entertainers became known as the "Borscht Belt."

Mexican Meatball Soup (*Sopa Albondigas*)

Adding cornmeal to the meatball mixture adds a distinctive flavor as well as serving the function of holding the meatballs together as they cook. Serve this hearty soup with some brown rice and a slaw made with a chile-laced dressing.

Makes 4 to 6 servings | Prep time: 20 minutes | Minimum cook time: 3 hours in a medium slow cooker

¾ pound ground beef

¾ pound ground pork

¼ cup yellow cornmeal

¼ cup milk

1 large egg, lightly beaten

2 tablespoons chili powder, divided

Salt and freshly ground black pepper to taste

2 tablespoons olive oil

1 large onion, diced

4 garlic cloves, minced

1 teaspoon ground cumin

½ teaspoon dried oregano

1 (28-ounce) can diced tomatoes, undrained

3 cups Beef Stock (page 23) or purchased stock

½ cup refrigerated commercial tomato salsa

2 tablespoons chopped fresh cilantro

Vegetable oil spray

1. Preheat the oven to 500°F. Line a broiler pan with heavy-duty aluminum foil, and grease the foil with vegetable oil spray.

2. Combine beef, pork, cornmeal, milk, egg, 1 tablespoon chili powder, salt, and pepper in a mixing bowl, and mix well. Form mixture into 1-inch balls, and place them on the greased foil. Brown meatballs in the oven for 10 minutes, or until lightly browned.

3. While meatballs brown, heat olive oil in a medium skillet over medium-high heat. Add onion and garlic, and cook, stirring frequently, for 3 minutes, or until onion is translucent. Reduce the heat to low, and stir in remaining 1 tablespoon chili powder, cumin, and oregano. Cook for 1 minute, stirring constantly. Scrape mixture into the slow cooker.

4. Add tomatoes, stock, salsa, and cilantro to the slow cooker, and stir well. Transfer meatballs to the slow cooker with a slotted spoon. Cook on Low for 6 to 8 hours or on High for 3 to 4 hours, or until meatballs are cooked through. Season to taste with salt and pepper, and serve hot.

Note: The soup can be prepared up to 3 days in advance and refrigerated, tightly covered. Reheat it, covered, over low heat, stirring occasionally.

Variation:

* Substitute ground turkey or chicken for the beef and pork, and substitute chicken stock for the beef stock.

The easiest way to break apart a whole head of garlic is to slam the root end onto the countertop. It should then separate easily.

Chinese Pork Soup with Rice Noodles

Main dish soups are common to all Asian cuisines, and this contains the heady aroma of toasted sesame oil along with the vegetables, which remain fairly crunchy even after cooking.

Makes 4 to 6 servings | Prep time: 20 minutes | Minimum cook time: 2 1/2 hours in a medium slow cooker

1 pound boneless pork loin

3 tablespoons soy sauce

2 tablespoons dry sherry

2 tablespoons Asian sesame oil, divided

1 tablespoon vegetable oil

4 scallions, white parts and 4 inches of green tops, sliced

3 garlic cloves, minced

1 tablespoon grated fresh ginger

4 cups chopped Napa or bok choy cabbage

5 cups Chicken Stock (page 21) or purchased stock

1 tablespoon rice wine vinegar

1 tablespoon granulated sugar

1 teaspoon Chinese chile paste with garlic, or to taste

5 ounces thick rice noodles

3 tablespoons chopped fresh cilantro

Salt and freshly ground black pepper to taste

1. Trim pork of all visible fat, and cut into very thin slices. Place pork into the slow cooker and toss it with soy sauce, sherry, and 1 tablespoon sesame oil.

2. Heat remaining sesame oil and vegetable oil in a small skillet over medium-high heat. Add scallions, garlic, and ginger. Cook, stirring constantly, for 30 seconds, or until fragrant. Scrape mixture into the slow cooker.

3. Add cabbage, stock, vinegar, sugar, and chile paste to the slow cooker, and stir well. Cook on Low for 4 1/2 to 6 hours or on High for 2 1/4 to 3 hours, or until pork is cooked through.

4. If cooking on Low, raise the heat to High. Add noodles and cilantro to soup, and season to taste with salt and pepper. Cook for an additional 15 to 20 minutes, or until noodles are soft and soup is bubbly. Serve immediately.

Note: The soup can be prepared up to 3 days in advance and refrigerated, tightly covered. Reheat it, covered, over low heat, stirring occasionally.

Variations:
* Substitute boneless, skinless chicken for the pork.
* Substitute extra-firm tofu for the pork, and substitute vegetable stock for the chicken stock.

Delicate and gluten-free rice noodles cook far faster than their wheat-based counterparts. In fact they really only need to soften. If making dishes with rice vermicelli, soaking it in hot tap water for less than 1 minute will do the trick, and for thicker noodles they need no more than a few minutes of simmering.

Italian Cabbage Soup with Sausage

Sausage should really be considered a convenience food because there are so many flavoring ingredients added to it during the grinding process. And all those flavors are then transferred to this hearty soup. Serve a tossed green salad with it, or a garlicky Caesar salad.

Makes 4 to 6 servings | Active time: 20 minutes | Minimum cook time: 3 1/2 hours in a medium slow cooker

¾ pound bulk sweet Italian sausage

1 medium onion, diced

2 garlic cloves, minced

2 carrots, diced

4 cups firmly packed thinly sliced green cabbage

5 cups Chicken Stock (page 21) or purchased stock

1 (14.5-ounce) can diced tomatoes, undrained

2 tablespoons tomato paste

1 pound redskin potatoes, scrubbed and cut into ¾-inch dice

2 tablespoons chopped fresh parsley

1 tablespoon chopped fresh oregano or 1 teaspoon dried

1 tablespoon chopped fresh thyme or ½ teaspoon dried

Salt and freshly ground black pepper to taste

1. Heat a skillet over medium-high heat. Add sausage and cook, breaking up lumps with a fork, for 3 to 5 minutes, or until sausage is browned. Remove sausage from the pan with a slotted spoon, and transfer it to the slow cooker. Discard all but 2 tablespoons fat from the skillet.

2. Add onion, garlic, and carrots to the skillet, and cook, stirring frequently, for 3 minutes, or until onion is translucent. Add cabbage, and cook for an additional 2 minutes, or until cabbage begins to wilt. Scrape mixture into the slow cooker.

3. Add stock, tomatoes, tomato paste, potatoes, parsley, oregano, and thyme to the slow cooker, and stir well. Cook on Low for 7 to 9 hours or on High for 3¹/₂ to 4¹/₂ hours, or until potatoes are tender. Season to taste with salt and pepper, and serve hot.

Note: The soup can be prepared up to 3 days in advance and refrigerated, tightly covered. Reheat it, covered, over low heat, stirring occasionally.

Variation:

✳ Substitute ground pork or ground beef for the sausage for a milder soup.

Like many recipes, this one calls for 2 tablespoons tomato paste. I buy tomato paste that comes in a tube, which will keep refrigerated for a few weeks. If you do open a can, freeze the remaining sauce in 1-tablespoon portions in an ice cube tray. Then store the small cubes in a heavy plastic bag for up to six months.

Chapter 4

From the Gardens and Plots:

Vegetarian Entrees

*M*ore and more people are now counting themselves amongst the ranks of the "occasional vegetarian" as we learn more about the need to replace large quantities of meats and their inherent saturated fats in our diets. One family of foods, legumes, have left the realm of the side dish and have become more important as entrees.

Beans are paired with rice or other grains in dishes around the world for more reasons than the flavor. What generations before us knew instinctively, and we now know scientifically, is that the protein in beans is "incomplete." This means that in order to deliver its best nutritional content and "complete" the protein, beans need to be paired with carbohydrate-rich grains such as rice or corn. Luckily these two major categories of grains are both gluten-free, and there are other options too in Chapter 8 to add grains to the beans. When the beans and grains are eaten together, they supply a quality of protein that's as good as that from eggs or beef.

A slow cooker is far more patient than any pot you would place on the stove, and due to the indirect heat there's no need to worry that the beans on the bottom are going to scorch and ruin the dish—a common pitfall to cooking beans conventionally. This shouldn't be surprising because slow cookers evolved from the old-fashioned bean pots of centuries past.

But you'll find a range of great recipes in this chapter beyond all things bean. The world of vegetables contains a panoply of flavors and colors. If you want to serve any of these dishes as a side dish, they will make about ten servings.

Moroccan Garbanzo Bean Stew

Most cuisines around the Mediterranean feature garbanzo beans. In the Middle East they're ground up with tahini to make hummus, and in both Italy and North Africa they're used extensively in soups and stews. This one has a vivid color to match its flavor and should be served over a grain such as buckwheat or rice.

Makes 4 to 6 servings | Prep time: 15 minutes | Minimum cook time: 3 1/2 hours in a medium slow cooker

2 cups dried garbanzo beans

3 tablespoons olive oil

2 large onions, diced

3 garlic cloves, minced

1 tablespoon ground cumin

2 teaspoons ground coriander

1 teaspoon turmeric

¼ teaspoon ground cinnamon

1 (28-ounce) can diced tomatoes, drained

4 cups Vegetable Stock (page 24) or purchased stock

Salt and freshly ground black pepper to taste

1. Rinse beans in a colander and place them in a mixing bowl covered with cold water. Allow beans to soak for at least 6 hours, or overnight. Or place beans into a saucepan and bring to a boil over high heat. Boil 1 minute. Turn off the heat, cover the pan, and soak beans for 1 hour. With either soaking method, drain beans, discard soaking water, and begin cooking as soon as possible.

2. Heat oil in a medium skillet over medium-high heat. Add onions and garlic, and cook, stirring frequently, for 3 minutes, or until onions are translucent. Reduce the heat to low, and stir in cumin, coriander, turmeric, and cinnamon. Cook for 1 minute, stirring constantly. Scrape mixture into the slow cooker.

3. Place drained beans in the slow cooker. Add tomatoes and stock, and stir well. Cook on Low for 7 to 8 hours or on High for 3 1/2 to 4 hours, or until garbanzo beans are tender. Season to taste with salt and pepper for the last hour of cooking time.

Note: The dish can be prepared up to 2 days in advance and refrigerated, tightly covered. Reheat it, covered, over low heat until hot, stirring occasionally.

Variation:

✳ Substitute lima beans for the garbanzo beans, and substitute 2 tablespoons Italian seasoning for the cumin, coriander, turmeric, and cinnamon.

> Turmeric is the root of a tropical plant, and it's what gives American mustard its distinctive yellow color. Turmeric is sometimes called "poor man's saffron" because it gives food a similar bright yellow color, but it doesn't have the same fragrance as saffron and it has a stronger flavor.

Vegetarian Hoppin' John

Like many Southern dishes, the traditional version of this black-eyed pea stew is made with ham hocks. You can gain the same nuances of hearty and smoky flavor in this recipe with the inclusion of a bit of Liquid Smoke, which is a natural product, not a chemical one, created from the distillation of hickory smoke. Serve this over rice.

Makes 4 to 6 servings | Prep time: 20 minutes | Minimum cook time: 4 hours in a medium slow cooker

1 pound dried black-eyed peas

2 tablespoons olive oil

2 large onions, diced

2 green bell peppers, seeds and ribs removed, and chopped

4 garlic cloves, minced

2 jalapeño or serrano chiles, seeds and ribs removed, and finely chopped

2½ cups Vegetable Stock (page 24) or purchased stock

¼ teaspoon Liquid Smoke

1 teaspoon dried thyme

2 bay leaves

Salt and freshly ground black pepper to taste

1. Rinse beans in a colander and place them in a mixing bowl covered with cold water. Allow beans to soak for at least 6 hours, or overnight. Or place beans into a saucepan and bring to a boil over high heat. Boil 1 minute. Turn off the heat, cover the pan, and soak beans for 1 hour. With either soaking method, drain beans, discard soaking water, and begin cooking as soon as possible.

2. Heat oil in a large skillet over medium-high heat. Add onions, green bell peppers, garlic, and chiles, and cook, stirring frequently, for 3 minutes, or until onions are translucent. Scrape mixture into the slow cooker.

3. Add drained beans to the slow cooker. Add stock, Liquid Smoke, thyme, and bay leaves. Stir well. Cook on Low for 8 to 10 hours or on High for 4 to 5 hours, or until beans are tender. Remove and discard bay leaves, season to taste with salt and pepper, and serve hot.

Note: The dish can be prepared up to 2 days in advance and refrigerated, tightly covered. Reheat it, covered, over low heat until hot, stirring occasionally.

Variation:

* Substitute kidney beans or pinto beans for the black-eyed peas, substitute 3 chipotle chiles in adobo sauce for the fresh chiles, and add 2 tablespoons chili powder and 2 teaspoons ground cumin to the slow cooker.

No self-respecting Southerner would start the New Year without eating a bowl of Hoppin' John. It's the regional good luck charm. The dish probably came from Africa, and it is mentioned in literature long before the Civil War. Some food authorities say the name comes from children hopping around the table on New Year's Day as a prelude to eating the dish.

Stewed Asian Black Beans

The black beans used most frequently in Asian cooking are either fermented with salt or ground up into a sauce. You'll find those flavors in this hearty stew, too, along other Asian condiments. Serve this over rice.

Makes 4 to 6 servings | Prep time: 15 minutes | Minimum cook time: 3 hours in a medium slow cooker

1½ cups dried black beans

2 tablespoons Asian sesame oil

8 scallions, white parts and 4 inches of green tops, cut into ½-inch pieces

3 garlic cloves, minced

2 tablespoons grated fresh ginger

5 cups Vegetable Stock (page 24) or purchased stock

½ cup dry sherry

¼ cup hoisin sauce

¼ cup tamari

2 tablespoons Chinese black bean sauce

2 tablespoons rice wine vinegar

2 teaspoons Chinese chile paste with garlic

2 teaspoons granulated sugar

Salt and freshly ground black pepper to taste

½ cup chopped fresh cilantro

1. Rinse beans in a colander and place them in a mixing bowl covered with cold water. Allow beans to soak for at least 6 hours, or overnight. Or place beans into a saucepan and bring to a boil over high heat. Boil 1 minute. Turn off the heat, cover the pan, and soak beans for 1 hour. With either soaking method, drain beans, discard soaking water, and begin cooking as soon as possible.

2. Heat sesame oil in a small skillet over medium-high heat. Add scallions, garlic, and ginger, and cook for 30 seconds, or until fragrant, stirring constantly. Scrape mixture into the slow cooker.

3. Place drained beans in the slow cooker. Add stock, sherry, hoisin sauce, tamari, black bean sauce, vinegar, chile paste, and sugar, and stir well. Cook on Low for 6 to 8 hours or on High for 3 to 4 hours, or until beans are tender. Season to taste with salt and pepper, stir in cilantro, and serve hot.

Note: The dish can be prepared up to 2 days in advance and refrigerated, tightly covered. Reheat it, covered, over low heat until hot, stirring occasionally.

Variation:

✳ Cut the beans back to 1 cup, and add ½ pound ground turkey to the slow cooker. Substitute chicken stock for the vegetable stock.

> You can prolong the life of leafy herbs like cilantro, parsley, and dill with good storage. Treat them like a bouquet of flowers; trim the stems when you get home from the market and then stand the bunch in a glass of water in the refrigerator.

Southwestern Spicy Kale and Pinto Bean Stew

Bright green kale makes a great addition for both color and flavor to this bean stew, which is on the table in a relatively short time because I developed it with canned beans. Serve it over brown or white rice.

Makes 4 to 6 servings | Prep time: 15 minutes | Minimum cook time: $1^1/_2$ hours in a medium slow cooker

1½ pounds kale

¼ cup olive oil

2 large onions, diced

3 garlic cloves, minced

2 green bell peppers, seeds and ribs removed, and chopped

2 jalapeño or serrano chiles, seeds and ribs removed, and finely chopped

2 tablespoons chili powder

1 tablespoon ground cumin

1 teaspoon dried oregano

1 bay leaf

2 (15-ounce) cans pinto beans, drained and rinsed

1 (28-ounce) cans diced tomatoes, undrained

2 cups Vegetable Stock (page 24) or purchased stock

3 tablespoons tomato paste

Salt and freshly ground black pepper to taste

1. Discard coarse stems from kale, then rinse and chop leaves. Place leaves in the slow cooker.

2. Heat oil in a small skillet over medium-high heat. Add onion, garlic, bell peppers, and chiles, and cook, stirring frequently, for 3 minutes, or until onion is translucent. Reduce the heat to low, and stir in chili powder, cumin, oregano, and bay leaf. Cook over low heat for 1 minute, stirring constantly. Scrape mixture into the slow cooker.

3. Add pinto beans, tomatoes, stock, and tomato paste to the slow cooker. Cook on Low for 3 to 5 hours or on High for $1^1/_2$ to 2 hours, or until kale is tender. Remove and discard bay leaf, season to taste with salt and pepper, and serve hot.

Note: The dish can be prepared up to 2 days in advance and refrigerated, tightly covered. Reheat it, covered, over low heat until hot, stirring occasionally.

Variation:

✳ Substitute Swiss chard or escarole for the kale.

> Kale is the pretty cousin in the cabbage family. Its flavor is very mild, and it has frilly deep green leaves that look like a bouquet of flowers rather than a tight head. Buy small heads that are perky and not limp.

Curried Red Lentil and Squash Stew

Lentils are a mainstay of the Indian diet, and because they require no pre-soaking and cook rather quickly this is not a stew that requires much advance planning. There's a bit of chile for some spice, and the zucchini adds both textural and visual interest. Serve this thick stew over some aromatic basmati rice for a full Indian experience.

Makes 4 to 6 servings | Prep time: 20 minutes | Minimum cook time: 2 hours in a medium slow cooker

¼ cup olive oil

2 medium onions, diced

3 garlic cloves, minced

1 jalapeño or serrano chile, seeds and ribs removed, and finely chopped

2 tablespoons curry powder

1 teaspoon ground cumin

1 teaspoon ground coriander

½ teaspoon turmeric

2 medium tomatoes, cored, seeded, and chopped

1½ cups red lentils

4 cups Vegetable Stock (page 24) or purchased stock

2 (3-inch) cinnamon sticks

2 cardamom pods

3 medium zucchini, cut into ¾-inch dice

¼ cup chopped fresh cilantro

Salt and freshly ground black pepper to taste

1. Heat oil in medium skillet over medium-high heat. Add onion, garlic, and chile pepper, and cook, stirring frequently, for 3 minutes, or until onion is translucent. Reduce the heat to low, and stir in curry powder, cumin, coriander, and turmeric. Cook for 1 minute, stirring constantly. Scrape mixture into the slow cooker.

2. Add tomatoes, lentils, stock, cinnamon sticks, and cardamom pods to the slow cooker, and stir well. Cook on Low for 3 to 5 hours or on High for 1½ to 2 hours, or until lentils are almost soft.

3. If cooking on Low, raise the heat to High. Remove and discard cinnamon sticks and cardamom pods, and add zucchini and cilantro to the slow cooker. Cook for 30 to 45 minutes, or until zucchini is tender. Season to taste with salt and pepper, and serve hot.

Note: The dish can be prepared up to 2 days in advance and refrigerated, tightly covered. Reheat it, covered, over low heat until hot, stirring occasionally.

Variation:

✻ Substitute yellow squash for the zucchini, and substitute green lentils for the red lentils.

Cardamom, an aromatic spice native to tropical countries, is a member of the ginger family. There are about 20 seeds in each dried pod, which are the size of a cranberry. The shells of the pods can be lightly crushed, and will disintegrate while the dish cooks—and, if not, they are easy to remove.

Zucchini Chili

Vegetarian chilis have become all the rage during the past decade, and I'm really fond of using zucchini as a stand-in for meat or poultry. Serve this with a tossed green salad over some brown rice.

Makes 4 to 6 servings | Prep time: 20 minutes | Minimum cook time: 3 hours in a medium slow cooker

3 small zucchini (about 1 pound)

2 tablespoons olive oil

1 large onion, diced

½ green or red bell pepper, seeds and ribs removed, and chopped

1 jalapeño or serrano chile, seeds and ribs removed, finely chopped

3 garlic cloves, minced

3 tablespoons chili powder

2 tablespoons smoked Spanish paprika

1 tablespoon ground cumin

2 teaspoon dried oregano

1 cup Vegetable Stock (page 24) or purchased stock

1 (15-ounce) can red kidney beans, drained and rinsed

1 (28-ounce) can crushed tomatoes in tomato puree

1 (4-ounce) can diced mild green chilies, drained

2 tablespoons tomato paste

1 tablespoon granulated sugar

Salt and freshly ground black pepper to taste

FOR SERVING:

Chopped scallions

Cilantro leaves

Sour cream or plain yogurt

Grated Monterey Jack cheese

1. Rinse and trim zucchini. Cut zucchini into quarters lengthwise, and then into ½-inch slices. Place slices in the slow cooker.

2. Heat oil in a medium skillet over medium-high heat. Add onion, bell pepper, chile, and garlic, and cook, stirring frequently, for 3 minutes, or until onion is translucent. Reduce the heat to low, and stir in chili powder, paprika, cumin, and oregano. Cook for 1 minute, stirring constantly. Scrape mixture into the slow cooker.

3. Add stock, kidney beans, tomatoes, green chilies, tomato paste, and sugar. Stir well. Cook on Low for 6 to 8 hours or on High for 3 to 4 hours, or until zucchini is tender. Season to taste with salt and pepper, and serve hot. Pass scallions, cilantro, sour cream, and cheese separately.

Note: The dish can be prepared up to 2 days in advance and refrigerated, tightly covered. Reheat it, covered, over low heat until hot, stirring occasionally.

Variation:

* Substitute yellow squash, green beans cut into 1½-inch segments, or chayote squash for the zucchini.

Zucchini is Italian in origin, and its native name was retained when it was integrated into American cooking. Choose small zucchini because they tend to have a sweeter flavor and the seeds are tender and less pronounced.

Spanish Vegetable Stew

This all-vegetable stew, made with vibrantly colored smoked paprika, is a variation on the caponata and ratatouille enjoyed in other parts of the Mediterranean. Serve it over Fontina Polenta (page 197) or brown rice.

Makes 4 to 6 servings | Prep time: 20 minutes | Minimum cook time: 2 1/2 hours in a medium slow cooker

1 (1-pound) eggplant

Salt

1/3 cup olive oil

1 large onion, diced

3 garlic cloves, minced

2 red bell peppers, seeds and ribs removed, and thinly sliced

2 tablespoons smoked Spanish paprika

small zucchini, cut into ¾-inch cubes

1 small summer squash, cut into ¾-inch cubes

1 (14.5-ounce) can crushed tomatoes

½ cup sliced green olives

1 cup Vegetable Stock (page 24) or purchased stock

2 tablespoons tomato paste

1 tablespoon chopped fresh oregano or 1 teaspoon dried

1 tablespoon fresh thyme or ½ teaspoon dried

Freshly ground black pepper to taste

1. Rinse and trim eggplant, and cut into ³/₄-inch cubes. Put eggplant in a colander, and sprinkle it liberally with salt. Place a plate on top of eggplant cubes, and weight the plate with cans. Place the colander in the sink or on a plate, and allow eggplant to drain for 30 minutes. Rinse eggplant cubes, and wring them dry with paper towels.

2. Heat half of oil in a medium skillet over medium-high heat. Add onion, garlic, and red bell peppers. Cook, stirring frequently, for 3 minutes, or until onion is translucent. Reduce the heat to low, stir in paprika, and cook over low heat for 1 minute, stirring constantly. Scrape mixture into the slow cooker.

3. Add remaining oil to the skillet, and add eggplant cubes. Cook, stirring frequently, for 3 minutes, or until eggplant begins to soften. Scrape eggplant into the slow cooker.

4. Add zucchini, summer squash, tomatoes, olives, stock, tomato paste, oregano, and thyme to the slow cooker. Stir well. Cook on Low for 5 to 7 hours or on High for 2¹/₂ to 3¹/₂ hours, or until vegetables are tender. Season to taste with salt and pepper, and serve hot.

Note: The dish can be prepared up to 2 days in advance and refrigerated, tightly covered. Reheat it, covered, over low heat until hot, stirring occasionally.

An easy way to cut bell peppers is to start by slicing off the bottom so the pepper sits flat on the cutting board. Then hold the pepper by its stem and slice down along the rounded curves between the indentations. The indentations are the ribs, so you end up with the ribs and seeds like a skeleton, which you can then discard.

Like tomatoes, eggplants are classified as fruits in botany, but we treat them as vegetables. Eggplants have male and female gender, and the males are preferable because they are less bitter and have fewer seeds. To tell a male from a female, look at the non-stem end. The male is rounded and has a more even hole; the female hole is indented.

Southern Vegetable Stew

Certain ingredients are almost synonymous with the best of Southern cooking, and that list includes sweet potato, okra, black-eyed peas, and corn. You'll find all of those plus lots of additional vegetables to add color and flavor in this hearty stew. Serve it over white or brown rice.

Makes 4 to 6 servings | *Prep time: 20 minutes* | *Minimum cook time: 3 hours in a medium slow cooker*

2 tablespoons olive oil

1 large onion, diced

3 garlic cloves, minced

2 celery ribs, sliced

1 green bell pepper, seeds and ribs removed, diced

1 small jalapeño or serrano chile, seeds and ribs removed, and finely chopped

2 tablespoons paprika

1 pound sweet potato, peeled and cut into ½-inch cubes

½ pound fresh okra, trimmed and cut into ½-inch slices

2 (14.5-ounce) cans diced tomatoes, undrained

2 cups Vegetable Stock (page 24) or purchased stock

3 tablespoons chopped fresh parsley

2 tablespoons chopped fresh oregano or 2 teaspoons dried

1 tablespoon fresh thyme or ½ teaspoon dried

2 bay leaves

1 (10-ounce) package frozen black-eyed peas, thawed

1 cup fresh corn kernels or frozen corn, thawed

Salt and hot red pepper sauce to taste

3 scallions, white parts and 3 inches of green tops, sliced

1. Heat oil in a medium skillet over medium-high heat. Add onion, garlic, celery, green bell pepper, and chile, and cook, stirring frequently, for 3 minutes, or until onion is translucent. Reduce the heat to low, stir in paprika, and cook for 1 minute, stirring constantly. Scrape mixture into the slow cooker.

2. Add sweet potato, okra, tomatoes, stock, parsley, oregano, thyme, and bay leaves to the slow cooker. Cook on Low for 5 to 7 hours or on High for 2½ to 3 hours, or until potatoes are almost tender.

3. If cooking on Low, raise the heat to High. Add black-eyed peas and corn. Cook for 30 to 45 minutes, or until vegetables are tender.

4. Remove and discard bay leaves, season to taste with salt and red pepper sauce, and serve hot, garnishing each serving with scallions.

Note: The dish can be prepared up to 2 days in advance and refrigerated, tightly covered. Reheat it, covered, over low heat until hot, stirring occasionally.

> Okra serves as a thickening agent as well as a vegetable in this stew. If fresh okra isn't available it's all right to substitute frozen okra, thawed. But add it along with the black-eyed peas and corn; it will fall apart if cooked longer.

Vegetarian Bolognese Sauce

With lots of fresh herbs and a good amount of red wine, this vegetarian sauce is just as hearty and flavorful as one made with meat. If not serving it to vegans, add some freshly grated Parmesan cheese on top.

Makes 6 to 8 servings | Prep time: 20 minutes | Minimum cook time: 3 hours in a medium slow cooker

¼ cup olive oil

1 large onion, diced

3 garlic cloves, minced

1 large red bell pepper, seeds and ribs removed, and diced

¾ pound mushrooms, wiped with a damp paper towel, trimmed, and sliced

1 large carrot, chopped

2 celery ribs, chopped

¼ cup chopped fresh parsley

2 tablespoons chopped fresh oregano or 2 teaspoons dried

2 tablespoons chopped fresh basil or 2 teaspoon dried

1 tablespoon chopped fresh rosemary or 1 teaspoon dried

2 bay leaves

2 (28-ounce) cans crushed tomatoes, undrained

1 cup dry red wine

3 tablespoons tomato paste

Salt and freshly ground black pepper to taste

1. Heat olive oil in a large skillet over medium-high heat. Add onion, garlic, bell pepper, and mushrooms, and cook, stirring frequently, for 5 to 7 minutes, or until mushrooms soften. Scrape mixture into the slow cooker.

2. Add carrot, celery, parsley, oregano, basil, rosemary, bay leaves, tomatoes, wine, and tomato paste to the slow cooker. Stir well.

3. Cook on Low for 6 to 8 hours or on High for 3 to 4 hours, or until vegetables are soft. Remove and discard bay leaves, season to taste with salt and pepper, and serve over gluten-free pasta.

Note: The dish can be prepared up to 2 days in advance and refrigerated, tightly covered. Reheat it, covered, over low heat until hot, stirring occasionally.

Variation:

✴ Substitute 1 (10-ounce) package frozen leaf spinach, thawed, for the red bell pepper.

If you've ever wondered why red bell peppers are always more expensive than green, it's because they are the same peppers, but they've been left on the plant to mature. That's why they're sweeter and less acidic than green peppers. But they are also more perishable to ship, which accounts for their premium price.

Chapter 5

From the Oceans and Lakes:

Fish and Seafood Entrees

When I first started working with slow cookers there were practically no fish recipes I felt were appropriate. But that's not the case. I had to reverse the order of when ingredients were added, at which time I realized that the slow cooker was as wonderful for aquatic species as ones living on land.

While chicken and meats are added to the slow cooker at the onset of cooking, or soon thereafter, fish and seafood is the last ingredient to be added to these recipes due to its short cooking time. Cubes of fish cook in mere minutes, while it can take cubes of beef up to 8 hours to reach tenderness. In fact, overcooking is a common mistake cooks make when handling seafood.

Another difference when cooking fish and seafood is that it does not freeze well—either before or after cooking. The reason is that when food is frozen the liquid inside the cells expand to form ice. This expansion punctures the delicate cell walls, which makes the fish mushy once thawed. So my suggestion is to double or even triple the recipe for the base *only*. Then freeze the extra portions of base. Thaw it when you come home, add the fresh fish, and within 10 minutes you'll be enjoying a delicious meal with perfectly cooked fish.

Secrets to Fish Selection

Fish fillets or steaks should look bright, lustrous, and moist, with no signs of discoloration or drying. Above all, do not buy any fish that actually smells fishy, indicating that it is no longer fresh or hasn't been cut or stored properly. Fresh fish has the mild, clean scent of the sea—nothing more. Look for bright, shiny colors in the fish scales, because as a fish sits, its skin becomes more pale and dull-looking. Then peer into the eyes; they should be black and beady. If they're milky or sunken, the fish has been dead too long. And if the fish isn't behind glass, gently poke its flesh. If the indentation remains, the fish isn't fresh enough.

It's more important to use the freshest fish in the market rather than a particular species. All fin fish fall into three basic families, and you can easily substitute one species for another. Use the following table to make life at the fish counter easier.

A Guide to Fish

DESCRIPTION	SPECIES	CHARACTERISTICS
Firm, lean	black sea bass, cod family, flat fish (flounder, sole, halibut), grouper, lingcod, ocean perch, perch, pike, porgy, red snapper, smelt, striped bass, turbot, salmon, trout, drum family, tilefish	low-fat, mild to delicate flavor, firm flesh, flakes when cooked
Meaty	catfish, carp, eel, monkfish (anglerfish), orange roughy, pike, salmon, shark, sturgeon, swordfish, some tuna varieties, mahi-mahi (dolphin fish), whitefish, pompano, yellowtail	low to high fat, diverse flavors and textures, usually thick steaks or fillets
Fatty or strong-flavored	bluefish, mackerel, some tuna varieties	high fat, pronounced flavor

Preparation Pointers

Rinse all fish under cold running water before cutting or cooking. With fillets, run your fingers in every direction along the top of the fillet before cooking, and feel for any pesky little bones.

You can remove bones easily in two ways. Larger bones will come out if they're stroked with a vegetable peeler, and you can pull out smaller bones with tweezers. This is not a long process, but it's a gesture that will be greatly appreciated by all who eat the fish.

To test for doneness, flake the fish with a fork; cooked fish will flake easily, and the color will be opaque rather than translucent. While cooking, fish flakes become milky and opaque from the outside in.

A vegetable peeler and a pair of tweezers are the best ways to get rid of those pesky little bones in fish fillets. Run a peeler down the center of the fillet, starting at the tail end. It will catch the larger pin bones, and with a twist of your wrist, you can pull them out. For finer bones, use your fingers to rub the flesh lightly and then pull out the bones with the tweezers.

Fish is high in protein and low to moderate in fat, cholesterol, and sodium. A 3-ounce portion of fish has between 47 and 170 calories, depending on the species, and is an excellent source of B vitamins, iodine, phosphorus, potassium, iron, and calcium. The most important nutrient in fish may be the omega-3 fatty acids. These are the primary polyunsaturated fatty acids found in the fat and oils of fish. They lower the levels of low-density lipoproteins (LDL, the "bad" cholesterol) and raise the levels of high-density lipoproteins (HDL, the "good" cholesterol). Fatty fish that live in cold water, such as mackerel and salmon, seem to have the most omega-3 fatty acids.

Paella

This all-in-one meal that originates in Valencia is perhaps one of Spain's best known dishes. The rice is aromatic and bright yellow from the use of saffron, and the seafood is nestled with vegetables. A tossed salad is all you need to complete the meal.

Makes 6 to 8 servings | Prep time: 20 minutes | Minimum cook time: 2 ¹/₂ hours in a medium slow cooker

2 tablespoons olive oil

1 large onion, diced

3 garlic cloves, minced

¹/₂ red bell pepper, seeds and ribs removed, and cut into ¹/₂-inch dice

2 cups long-grain converted rice

4 cups Seafood Stock (page 25) or purchased stock

3 tablespoons chopped fresh parsley

1 tablespoon chopped fresh oregano or 1 teaspoon dried

1 tablespoon fresh thyme or ¹/₂ teaspoon dried

1 bay leaf

¹/₂ teaspoon crushed saffron threads

Salt and freshly ground black pepper to taste

1 cup frozen peas, thawed

³/₄ pound extra-large (16 to 20 per pound) raw shrimp, peeled and deveined

¹/₂ pound sea scallops, rinsed and halved

¹/₂ pound swordfish, or other thick firm-fleshed white fish fillet, rinsed and cut into 1-inch cubes

1. Heat oil in a medium skillet over medium-high heat. Add onion, garlic, and bell pepper. Cook, stirring frequently, for 3 minutes, or until onion is translucent. Scrape mixture into the slow cooker.

2. Add rice, stock, parsley, oregano, thyme, bay leaf, and saffron to the slow cooker, and stir well. Cook on Low for 4 to 6 hours or on High for 2 to 3 hours, or until rice is almost tender.

3. If cooking on Low, raise the heat to High. Season mixture to taste with salt and pepper, remove and discard bay leaf, and stir in peas, shrimp, scallops, and swordfish. Cook for an additional 30 to 45 minutes, or until shrimp are pink and fish is cooked through.

Note: The dish can be prepared up to 2 days in advance and refrigerated, tightly covered. Reheat it, covered, in a 350°F oven for 20 to 25 minutes, or until hot.

Variations:

✳ Add 1 (10-ounce) package frozen artichoke hearts, thawed, along with the peas and seafood.

✳ Add ³/₄ pound boneless, skinless chicken meat, cut into 1-inch cubes, to the dish at the onset of the cooking time.

On a per ounce basis, saffron, rather than caviar or fresh white truffles, is the most expensive food in the world. All the threads are harvested individually by hand from the purple crocus. Saffron was once used not only for cooking but also in making medicines and dyeing cloth that characteristic yellow color. Saffron from Spain is less expensive than Asian saffron.

Shrimp Creole

The Creole cuisine of Louisiana is an amalgam of French, Italian, and Spanish influences tempered with African-American, and shrimp Creole is one of its premier dishes. The tomato sauce is laced with garlic and herbs, and the Holy Trinity of Creole cooking—scallions, celery, and green bell pepper. A crunchy slaw is a good choice to accompany this dish, which should be served over rice.

Makes 4 to 6 servings | Prep time: 20 minutes | Minimum cook time: 2 1/2 hours in a medium slow cooker

3 tablespoons olive oil

6 scallions, white parts and 3 inches of green tops, chopped

2 celery ribs, sliced

½ green bell pepper, seeds and ribs removed, and finely diced

3 garlic cloves, minced

1 tablespoon dried oregano

1 tablespoon paprika

1 teaspoon ground cumin

½ teaspoon dried basil

1 (15-ounce) can tomato sauce

½ cup Seafood Stock (page 25) or purchased stock

2 bay leaves

1½ pound extra-large (16 to 20 per pound) raw shrimp, peeled and deveined

Salt and cayenne to taste

1. Heat oil in a medium skillet over medium-high heat. Add scallions, celery, bell pepper, and garlic. Cook, stirring frequently, for 3 minutes, or until scallions are translucent. Reduce the heat to low, and stir in oregano, paprika, cumin, and basil. Cook 1 minute, stirring constantly. Scrape mixture into the slow cooker.

2. Add tomato sauce, stock, and bay leaves to the slow cooker, and stir well. Cook on Low for 4 to 6 hours or on High for 2 to 3 hours, or until vegetables are soft.

3. If cooking on Low, raise the heat to High. Remove and discard bay leaves, and stir in shrimp. Cook for 15 to 30 minutes, or until shrimp are pink and cooked through. Season to taste with salt and cayenne, and serve hot.

Note: The dish can be prepared up to 2 days in advance and refrigerated, tightly covered. Reheat it, covered, over low heat until hot, stirring occasionally.

Variation:

* Substitute bay scallops, sea scallops cut into quarters, or 1-inch cubes of firm-fleshed white fish for the shrimp.

Do not equate the words "fresh shrimp" with shrimp that have never been frozen. Truth be told, you probably will be unable to find never-frozen shrimp fresh from the ocean these days unless you have a shrimper friend or net it yourself. This is not necessarily a bad thing. Nowadays, shrimp is harvested, cleaned, and flash frozen on the boats before they ever reach the shore. But if you plan to freeze shrimp, ask the fishmonger to sell you some still frozen rather than thawed in the case.

Caribbean Curried Fish

Creamy coconut milk tones down the fiery chile and curry in this delicious stew flecked with black beans, which should be served over rice. My first choice of fish species for this dish is grouper, but I know that finding that Caribbean stalwart is not easy in northern climates, so use the chart on page 98 for other ideas.

Makes 4 to 6 servings | Prep time: 15 minutes | Minimum cook time: 3 1/2 hours in a medium slow cooker

2 tablespoons olive oil

2 medium onions, diced

4 garlic cloves, minced

1 jalapeño or Scotch bonnet chile, seeds and ribs removed, and finely chopped

2 tablespoons curry powder

1 tablespoon ground cumin

3 ripe plum tomatoes, cored and diced

2 (14-ounce) cans light coconut milk

1 (15-ounce) can black beans, drained and rinsed well

1 cup fresh peas or frozen peas, thawed

1½ pounds grouper or other thick firm-fleshed white fish, rinsed, cut into 1-inch cubes

Salt and freshly ground black pepper to taste

1. Heat oil in a medium skillet over medium-high heat. Add onions, garlic, and chile. Cook, stirring frequently, for 3 minutes, or until onion is translucent. Reduce the heat to low, and stir in curry powder and cumin. Cook for 1 minute, stirring constantly. Scrape mixture into the slow cooker.

2. Add tomatoes and coconut milk to the slow cooker, and stir well. Cook on Low for 6 to 8 hours or on High for 3 to 4 hours, or until vegetables are soft.

3. If cooking on Low, raise the heat to High. Stir in beans, peas, and fish. Cook for 25 to 35 minutes, or until fish is cooked through and flakes easily. Season to taste with salt and pepper, and serve hot.

Note: The dish can be prepared up to 2 days in advance and refrigerated, tightly covered. Reheat it, covered, over low heat until hot, stirring occasionally.

Variation:

✳ Substitute extra-large shrimp (16 to 20 per pound) or bay scallops for the fish.

There's very little difference in taste or texture between light coconut milk and the high-test variety, but using the light version cuts down substantially on fat, which then cuts down substantially on the calories.

Fish Veracruz

People seem to lose sight of the fact that most of Mexico is bounded by coastline because so much of our beloved Tex-Mex food is based on dishes from landlocked Sonora province. This delicate fish in a spicy sauce tomato sauce is wonderful served either over rice or with corn tortillas.

Makes 4 to 6 servings | Prep time: 15 minutes | Minimum cook time: 2¹/₂ hours in a medium slow cooker

2 tablespoons olive oil

2 onions, thinly sliced

4 garlic cloves, minced

1 jalapeño or serrano chile, seeds and ribs removed, and finely chopped

1 tablespoon chili powder

2 teaspoons dried oregano, preferably Mexican

1 (14.5-ounce) can diced tomatoes, undrained

1 cup Seafood Stock (page 25) or purchased stock

2 tablespoons freshly squeezed lemon juice

2 tablespoons tomato paste

1 teaspoon grated lemon zest

¼ cup sliced green olives

1½ pounds red snapper or other firm-fleshed white fish fillets, cut into serving pieces

Salt and freshly ground black pepper to taste

1. Heat oil in a medium skillet over medium-high heat. Add onions, garlic, and chile, and cook, stirring frequently, for 3 minutes, or until onions are translucent. Reduce the heat to low, and stir in chili powder and oregano. Cook for 1 minute, stirring constantly. Scrape mixture into the slow cooker.

2. Add tomatoes, stock, lemon juice, tomato paste, and lemon zest to the slow cooker, and stir well. Cook for 4 to 6 hours on Low or for 2 to 3 hours on High, or until vegetables are tender.

3. If cooking on Low, raise the heat to High. Stir in olives, and gently add fish. Cook for 20 to 40 minutes, or until fish is cooked through and flakes easily. Season to taste with salt and pepper, and serve hot.

Note: The dish can be prepared up to 2 days in advance and refrigerated, tightly covered. Reheat it, covered, in a 350°F oven for 20 to 25 minutes, or until hot.

Variations:

* Substitute 4 to 6 (4-ounce) boneless, skinless chicken breasts for the fish and substitute chicken stock for the seafood stock. Add the chicken at the onset of the cooking time, and add 1 hour if cooking on Low and 30 minutes if cooking on High.
* Substitute extra-large (16 to 20 per pound) raw shrimp, peeled and deveined, for the fish.

Chili powder, like Italian seasoning, is a pre-mixed blend of herbs and spices; if you make it yourself, you can personalize the taste to suit your own. The base should be ground red chiles and ground cumin. Then add as much paprika, ground coriander, cayenne, and oregano as you like. Some brands also include garlic powder and onion powder.

Spicy Southwest Shrimp

This dish could be dubbed "shrimp chili." It has lots of seasonings plus beans and tomatoes, and extra zest from the inclusion of spicy chorizo sausage. Serve it over rice with some pico de gallo or sliced jicama.

Makes 4 to 6 servings | Prep time: 15 minutes | Minimum cook time: 2 1/2 hours in a medium slow cooker

¼ pound bulk raw chorizo sausage

2 medium onions, diced

5 garlic cloves, minced

2 jalapeño or serrano chiles, seeds and ribs removed, and finely chopped

1 tablespoon paprika

1 tablespoon ground cumin

2 medium tomatoes, cored, seeded, and diced

2 (15-ounce) cans red kidney beans, drained and rinsed

2½ cups Seafood Stock (page 25) or purchased stock

2 tablespoons chopped fresh oregano or 2 teaspoons dried

1 tablespoon fresh thyme or ½ teaspoon dried

1½ pound extra-large (16 to 20 per pound) raw shrimp, peeled and deveined

3 tablespoons chopped fresh cilantro

Salt and freshly ground black pepper to taste

1. Heat a skillet over medium-high heat. Crumble sausage into the skillet, and cook, stirring frequently, until sausage browns. Remove sausage from the skillet with a slotted spoon, and place it in the slow cooker. Add onions, garlic, and chiles to the skillet, and cook, stirring frequently, for 3 minutes, or until onions are translucent. Reduce the heat to low, and stir in paprika and cumin. Cook for 1 minute, stirring constantly. Scrape mixture into the slow cooker.

2. Add tomatoes, beans, stock, oregano, and thyme to the slow cooker, and stir well. Cook on Low for 4 to 6 hours or on High for 2 to 3 hours, or until vegetables are soft.

3. If cooking on Low, raise the heat to High. Stir in shrimp and cilantro, and cook for 15 to 30 minutes, or until shrimp are pink and cooked through. Season to taste with salt and pepper, and serve hot.

Note: The dish can be prepared up to 2 days in advance and refrigerated, tightly covered. Reheat it, covered, over low heat until hot, stirring occasionally.

Variation:

✳ Substitute vegetable stock for the seafood stock, and substitute 1-inch cubes of extra-firm tofu for the shrimp.

Devein means to remove the black vein, actually the intestinal tract, from shrimp. Do this with the tip of a sharp paring knife or with a specialized tool called a *deveiner*.

Lemony Greek Fish Stew

The delectable combination of lemon, garlic, and oregano is one of the hallmarks of Greek cuisine, and those are the flavors you'll find in this light and flavorful fish stew. A Greek salad made with sharp feta cheese is a good choice to complete the meal.

Makes 4 to 6 servings | Active time: 15 minutes | Minimum cook time: 4 hours in a medium slow cooker

3 tablespoons olive oil

1 medium onion, diced

3 garlic cloves, minced

2 celery ribs, sliced

¼ cup chopped fresh parsley

2 tablespoons dried oregano

1 bay leaf

2 cups Seafood Stock (page 25) or purchased stock

¾ cup dry white wine

¼ cup freshly squeezed lemon juice

1 pound redskin potatoes, scrubbed and cut into ¾-inch dice

2 small zucchini, halved lengthwise, and thinly sliced

1½ pounds thick white fish fillet, rinsed and cut into 1-inch cubes

Salt and freshly ground black pepper to taste

1 tablespoon cornstarch

Salt and freshly ground black pepper to taste

1. Heat olive oil in a small skillet over medium-high heat. Add onion, garlic, and celery, and cook, stirring frequently, for 3 minutes, or until onion is translucent. Scrape mixture into the slow cooker.

2. Add parsley, oregano, bay leaf, stock, wine, lemon juice, and potatoes to the slow cooker, and stir well. Cook on Low for 6 to 8 hours or on High for 3 to 4 hours, or until vegetables are almost soft.

3. If cooking on Low, raise the heat to High. Add zucchini and fish, and cook for 30 to 40 minutes, or until fish is cooked through and flakes easily. Remove and discard bay leaf, and season to taste with salt and pepper.

4. Mix cornstarch with water, and stir cornstarch mixture into the slow cooker. Cook for an additional 10 to 20 minutes, or until juices are bubbling and slightly thickened. Serve immediately.

Note: The dish can be prepared up to 2 days in advance and refrigerated, tightly covered. Reheat it, covered, over low heat until hot, stirring occasionally.

Variation:

∗ Substitute chicken stock for the seafood stock, and substitute 1½ pounds boneless, skinless chicken, cut into ¾-inch dice, for the fish. Add the chicken at the onset of the cooking time.

> To get the maximum amount of juice from citrus fruits, roll them back and forth on a counter or prick the skin and microwave them on high power for 30 seconds.

Szechwan Scallops in Black Bean Sauce

The use of pungent fermented black beans along with the traditional mix of garlic, ginger, and scallions gives this dish a vibrant flavor. Serve it with some stir-fried vegetables and aromatic jasmine rice.

Makes 4 to 6 servings | Prep time: 15 minutes | Minimum cook time: 2 hours in a medium slow cooker

3 tablespoons Chinese fermented black beans, coarsely chopped but not rinsed

1/3 cup dry sherry

6 scallions, white parts and 4 inches of green tops, thinly sliced

2 tablespoons Asian sesame oil

4 garlic cloves, minced

3 tablespoons grated fresh ginger

1/2 pound bok choy, cut into 1/2-inch slices

2 cups Seafood Stock (page 25) or purchased stock

3 tablespoons soy sauce

3 tablespoons Chinese oyster sauce

2 teaspoons Chinese chile paste with garlic

1 1/2 pounds bay scallops or sea scallops cut into quarters

1 tablespoon cornstarch

Salt and freshly ground black pepper to taste

1. Stir black beans into sherry to plump for 10 minutes. Reserve 3 tablespoons scallions. Heat sesame oil in a small skillet over medium-high heat. Add remaining scallions, garlic, and ginger, and cook for 30 seconds, stirring constantly, or until fragrant. Scrape mixture into the slow cooker.

2. Add bok choy, sherry mixture, stock, soy sauce, oyster sauce, and chile paste to the slow cooker, and stir well. Cook on Low for 3 to 5 hours or on High for 1 1/2 to 2 hours, or until vegetables are crisp-tender.

3. If cooking on Low, raise the heat to High. Stir in scallops, and cook for 15 to 30 minutes, or until scallops are cooked through. Mix cornstarch and 2 tablespoons cold water in a small cup, and stir cornstarch mixture into the slow cooker. Cook for an additional 5 to 10 minutes, or until juices are bubbling and slightly thickened.

4. Season to taste with salt and pepper. Sprinkle with remaining 3 tablespoons scallions, and serve hot.

Note: The dish can be prepared up to 2 days in advance and refrigerated, tightly covered. Reheat it, covered, over low heat until hot, stirring occasionally.

Variations:

* Substitute 1-inch cubes of cod, halibut, or any firm-fleshed white fish, or extra-large shrimp for the scallops.

* Substitute 3/4-inch cubes of boneless, skinless chicken breast for the scallops, and substitute chicken stock for the seafood stock. Add chicken along with the vegetables at the beginning of the cooking time.

Fermented black beans are small black soybeans with a pungent flavor that have been preserved in salt before being packed. They should be chopped and soaked in some sort of liquid to soften them and release their flavor prior to cooking. Because they are salted as a preservative, they last for up to 2 years if refrigerated once opened. Most supermarkets now carry them, but if you have an Asian market in your neighborhood buy them there because they'll be less expensive.

Moroccan Fish Tagine

A tagine might sound exotic, but it's basically a Moroccan stew that can feature just about any sort of fish, meat, or poultry as long as there are olives and spices such as cumin included in the mix. Serve this with rice or Kasha (page 205) and a salad made with a lemony dressing.

Makes 4 to 6 servings | Prep time: 15 minutes | Minimum cook time: 2 1/2 hours in a medium slow cooker

1½ pounds cod, halibut, or other firm-fleshed white fish, cut into serving pieces

⅔ cup olive oil, divided

¼ cup freshly squeezed lemon juice

¼ cup dry white wine

2 tablespoons chopped fresh cilantro

1 tablespoon paprika

1 teaspoon ground cumin

1 teaspoon ground ginger

Salt and cayenne to taste

2 large onions, diced

3 garlic cloves, minced

1 cup Seafood Stock (page 25) or purchased stock

½ cup sliced pimiento-stuffed green olives

2 bay leaves

Freshly ground black pepper to taste

1. Rinse fish fillets and set aside. Combine ½ cup oil, lemon juice, wine, cilantro, paprika, cumin, ginger, salt, and cayenne in a heavy, resealable plastic bag. Mix well and add fish. Marinate fish refrigerated for 2 to 4 hours, turning the bag occasionally so fish marinates evenly.

2. Heat remaining oil in a medium skillet over medium-high heat. Add onions and garlic, and cook, stirring frequently, for 3 minutes, or until onions are translucent. Scrape mixture into the slow cooker.

3. Drain marinade from fish, and add liquid to the slow cooker, along with stock, olives, and bay leaves. Stir well. Return fish to the bag, and refrigerate. Cook on Low for 4 to 5 hours or on High for 2 to 3 hours, or until onion is tender.

4. If cooking on Low, raise the heat to High. Add fish to the slow cooker, and cook for 30 to 40 minutes, or until fish is cooked through and flakes easily. Remove and discard bay leaves, season to taste with salt and pepper, and serve hot.

Note: The dish can be prepared up to 2 days in advance and refrigerated, tightly covered. Reheat it, covered, over low heat until hot, stirring occasionally.

Variation:

∗ Substitute vegetable stock for the seafood stock and substitute thick slices of firm tofu for the fish.

Paprika is a powder made by grinding aromatic sweet red pepper pods several times. The color can vary from deep red to bright orange, and the flavor ranges from mild to pungent and hot. Hungarian cuisine is characterized by paprika as a flavoring, and Hungarian paprika is considered the best product.

Rare Salmon with Salsa Topping

As soon as I started reading about chefs cooking fish in a 200°F oven I knew that the slow cooker would be even better! This robust fish remains perfectly rare and the salsa is a great topping. (As they do on restaurant menus, I feel obligated to tell you that some health authorities warn against eating uncooked and undercooked fish and seafood along with meats. Okay, I've just given you the warning.)

Makes 4 to 6 servings | Prep time: 15 minutes | Minimum cook time: 1 hour in a medium slow cooker

4 to 6 (6-ounce) salmon steaks, at least ¾-inch thick

3 tablespoons olive oil, divided

3 garlic cloves, minced

2 tablespoons ground cumin

2 tablespoons chili powder

Salt and freshly ground black pepper to taste

4 ripe plum tomatoes, cored, and chopped

3 scallions, white parts and 3 inches of green tops, chopped

3 tablespoons snipped fresh chives

2 tablespoons freshly squeezed lime juice

1. Rub salmon with 1 tablespoon olive oil. Combine garlic, cumin, chili powder, salt, and pepper in a small bowl. Rub mixture on both sides of salmon.

2. Combine remaining olive oil with tomatoes, scallions, chives, and lime juice. Season to taste with salt and pepper.

3. Place salmon in the slow cooker. Cook on High for 40 minutes. Turn salmon gently with a slotted spatula. Top salmon with tomato mixture, and cook on High for an additional 20 to 30 minutes for rare, or longer for fish that is better done. Serve immediately.

Note: This dish should not be prepared in advance and reheated. Make it just prior to serving.

Variation:

✳ Substitute tuna steaks for the salmon.

> You can always substitute finely chopped green scallion tops for chives in any recipe. It's rare that you ever use a whole scallion, so they frequently go to waste.

Caponata Fish Sauce

Caponata is a traditional Italian vegetable dish, and in this case the addition of fish transforms a side dish into a vibrant sauce for gluten-free pasta flecked with olives and capers. Serve a tossed salad with a garlicky dressing along with it.

Makes 4 to 6 servings | Active time: 20 minutes | Minimum cook time: 3 1/2 hours in a medium slow cooker

1 (1-pound) eggplant, cut into ¾-inch cubes

Salt and freshly ground black pepper

⅓ cup olive oil, divided

2 celery ribs, diced

1 medium onion, diced

½ red bell pepper, seeds and ribs removed, and diced

4 garlic cloves, minced

¼ cup red wine vinegar

2 tablespoons granulated sugar

1 (14.5-ounce) can diced tomatoes, undrained

1 (15-ounce) can tomato sauce

1 cup Seafood Stock (page 25) or purchased stock

2 tablespoons capers, rinsed

¼ cup raisins

1½ pounds cod, halibut, or any thick firm white-fleshed fish fillet, cut into 1-inch cubes

1. Place eggplant in a colander, and sprinkle cubes liberally with salt. Place a plate on top of eggplant cubes, and weight the plate with some cans. Place the colander in the sink or on a plate, and allow eggplant to drain for 30 minutes. Rinse eggplant cubes, and squeeze hard to remove water. Wring out remaining water with a cloth tea towel.

2. Heat ¹/₂ of olive oil in large skillet over medium-high heat. Add onions, celery, bell pepper, and garlic, and cook, stirring frequently, for 3 minutes, or until onion is translucent. Scrape mixture into the slow cooker.

3. Return the pan to the stove, and heat remaining olive oil over medium-high heat. Add eggplant cubes and cook, stirring frequently, for 3 minutes, or until cubes are lightly browned. Scrape eggplant into the slow cooker, and stir in vinegar, sugar, tomatoes, tomato sauce, stock, capers, and raisins.

4. Cook on Low for 5 to 6 hours or on High for 2¹/₂ to 3 hours, or until vegetables are almost soft.

5. If cooking on Low, raise the heat to High. Add fish and cook for 20 to 40 minutes, or until fish is cooked through and flakes easily. Season to taste with salt and pepper, and serve hot.

Note: The dish can be prepared up to 2 days in advance and refrigerated, tightly covered. Reheat it, covered, over low heat until hot, stirring occasionally.

Variation:

✳ Substitute 3 (5-ounce) cans of solid white tuna packed in water, drained and broken into chunks, for the fish. The tuna only has to cook for 10 to 20 minutes, or until hot.

> Capers are the flower bud of a low bush native to the Mediterranean. After harvest they're sun-dried and pickled in vinegar. The best capers are the tiny ones from France. Although they're customarily packed in brine, you can also find them packed in coarse salt. However you buy them, rinse them well before using.

Chapter 6

From the Coops and Barnyards:
Poultry Entrees

*I*f you're like most Americans, it's a safe bet that roughly three nights a week you're having some form of chicken for dinner.

But how times have changed! In the seventeenth century, King Henry IV of France's Prime Minister Sully used "a chicken in every pot" as a metaphor for the prosperity he wished for his citizens. In the 1600s, chickens then were associated with luxury rather than with fast food. Today chicken is the food that dominates the center of Americans' plates, with per capita consumption now topping 90 pounds. That figure has more than doubled since 1970, and beef consumption has declined as a result.

Why has the little bird eclipsed the big cow? There are many reasons, including its lower cost and its nutritional profile. Chicken is healthier than red meats, discounting the saturated fat in the skin. It also takes to myriad preparation methods, including the "wet heat" recipes that utilize the slow cooker.

Safety First

Poultry should always be rinsed under cold running water after being taken out of the package. If it's going to be pre-browned in the oven or in a skillet on the stove, pat the pieces dry with paper towels and then wash your hands. Chicken often contains salmonella, a naturally occurring bacterium that is killed by cooking, but you don't want to transfer this bacterium to other foods.

For the sake of food safety, it's best not to cook a whole chicken in the slow cooker, because the low heat might keep the meat of a whole bird in the bacterial danger zone for more than two hours.

For braised chicken dishes, I advocate using thighs, legs, and breasts, which can be cut in half. They're bigger than the other pieces and they fit more neatly in the slow cooker if cut. Save the wings separately for making baked or grilled wings for a picnic or snack; there's not enough meat on them to justify taking up room in the slow cooker.

For stews made with boneless, skinless meat, use breasts, thighs, or a combination. I think the dark meat has more flavor, but if you prefer breasts, use them.

Pollo Cubano

Heady dark rum and fresh ginger are accents in this Caribbean sweet and sour chicken dish. Serve it with some rice and stewed beans.

Makes 4 to 6 servings | Prep time: 15 minutes | Minimum cook time: 3 ¼ hours in a medium slow cooker

1 (3- to 4-pound) chicken, cut into serving pieces, or 6 chicken pieces of your choice

3 tablespoons olive oil

2 large onions, halved and thinly sliced

3 garlic cloves, minced

3 tablespoons grated fresh ginger

1¼ cups Chicken Stock (page 21) or purchased stock

½ cup cider vinegar

½ cup dark rum

½ cup firmly packed dark brown sugar

1½ tablespoons cornstarch

Salt and freshly ground black pepper to taste

1. Rinse chicken and pat dry with paper towels. Preheat the oven broiler, and line a broiler pan with heavy-duty aluminum foil. Broil chicken pieces for 3 minutes per side, or until browned.

2. Heat oil in a large skillet over medium-high heat. Add onion, garlic, and ginger, and cook, stirring frequently, for 3 minutes, or until onion is translucent. Scrape mixture into the slow cooker.

3. Add stock, vinegar, rum, and brown sugar to the slow cooker, and stir well. Arrange chicken pieces in the slow cooker, skin side down. Cook on Low for 6 to 8 hours or on High for 3 to 4 hours, or until chicken is cooked through, tender, and no longer pink.

4. If cooking on Low, raise the heat to High. Mix cornstarch with 2 tablespoons cold water in a small cup, and stir cornstarch mixture into the juices in the slow cooker. Cook for an additional 15 to 20 minutes, or until juices are bubbling and slightly thickened. Season to taste with salt and pepper, and serve hot.

Note: The dish can be prepared up to 2 days in advance and refrigerated, tightly covered. Reheat it, covered, in a 350°F oven for 20 to 25 minutes, or until hot.

Variation:

❊ Substitute 4 to 6 (6-ounce) boneless pork chops for the chicken.

Unless brown sugar is stored in an airtight container the moisture from the molasses can evaporate and the sugar turns into a rock. But there's no need to throw it away. Add a few slices of apple and close the bag securely. In a day or so, the sugar will have softened again. If you need to use some immediately, chip off some of the hard sugar and dissolve it in water.

Coq au Vin

This dish of chicken cooked in red wine with mushrooms and pearl onions is a classic French bistro dish, and it is traditionally served with steamed new potatoes. Accompany it with a green vegetable such as green beans or asparagus.

Makes 4 to 6 servings | Prep time: 20 minutes | Minimum cook time: 3 1/4 hours in a medium slow cooker

1 (3- to 4-pound) chicken, cut into serving pieces, or 6 chicken pieces of your choice

½ pound white or crimini mushrooms

2 cups dry red wine

½ cup Chicken Stock (page 21) or purchased stock

1 tablespoon brandy

3 garlic cloves, minced

3 tablespoons chopped fresh parsley

1 tablespoon fresh thyme or ½ teaspoon dried

1 bay leaf

1 (1-pound) bag frozen pearl onions, thawed

1 tablespoon cornstarch

Salt and freshly ground black pepper to taste

1. Rinse chicken and pat dry with paper towels. Preheat the oven broiler, and line a broiler pan with heavy-duty aluminum foil. Broil chicken pieces for 3 minutes per side, or until browned. Wipe mushrooms with a damp paper towel. Trim the stems, and cut in half if large.

2. Add wine, stock, brandy, garlic, parsley, thyme, bay leaf, pearl onions, and mushrooms to the slow cooker, and stir well. Arrange chicken pieces in the slow cooker, skin side down.

3. Cook on Low for 6 to 8 hours or on High for 3 to 4 hours, or until chicken is cooked through, tender, and no longer pink. Remove chicken and vegetables from the cooker with a slotted spoon, and cover with foil to keep warm.

4. Pour cooking liquid from the slow cooker into a saucepan, and bring it to a boil over high heat. Boil until liquid is reduced in volume by half. Mix cornstarch and 2 tablespoons cold water in a small cup, and add cornstarch mixture to the boiling liquid. Reduce the heat to low, and simmer the sauce for 2 minutes, or until juices are bubbling and slightly thickened. Remove and discard bay leaf, season to taste with salt and pepper, and pour sauce over chicken.

Note: The dish can be prepared up to 2 days in advance and refrigerated, tightly covered. Reheat it, covered, in a 350°F oven for 20 to 25 minutes, or until hot.

Variations:

✳ Substitute dry white wine for the red wine, and add 2 tablespoons grated lemon zest.

✳ Cook ¼ pound bacon, cut into 1-inch segments, until crisp. Add it to the slow cooker along with the chicken.

> When cooking with wine or any other acid such as lemon juice, it's important to use a stainless-steel or coated steel pan rather than aluminum. When mixed with the wine or acid, an aluminum pan can impart a metallic taste to the dish.

Chicken à la Normande

Many delicate dishes native to the Normandy region of France join apples and the region's famed apple brandy with cream, and this is one of them. It's a great fall dish, especially with some Braised Red Cabbage (page 213) and rice or steamed potatoes.

Makes 4 to 6 servings | Prep time: 20 minutes | Minimum cook time: 3 1/4 hours in a medium slow cooker

1 (3- to 4-pound) chicken, cut into serving pieces, or 6 chicken pieces of your choice

2 Granny Smith apples

1½ cups Chicken Stock (page 21) or purchased stock

⅓ cup dry white wine

2 tablespoons Calvados or other apple brandy

3 tablespoons firmly packed light brown sugar

2 tablespoons chopped fresh parsley

1 tablespoon fresh chopped thyme or ½ teaspoon dried

1½ tablespoons cornstarch

½ cup heavy cream

Salt and freshly ground black pepper to taste

1. Rinse chicken and pat dry with paper towels. Preheat the oven broiler, and line a broiler pan with heavy-duty aluminum foil. Broil chicken pieces for 3 minutes per side, or until browned. Peel and core apples. Cut each apple into 6 pieces.

2. Add stock, wine, Calvados, brown sugar, parsley, and thyme to the slow cooker, and stir well. Arrange apple slices and chicken pieces in the slow cooker, skin side down. Cook on Low for 6 to 8 hours or on High for 3 to 4 hours, or until chicken is cooked through, tender, and no longer pink.

3. If cooking on Low, raise the heat to High. Stir cornstarch into cream, and stir cornstarch mixture into the slow cooker. Cook for an additional 15 to 20 minutes, or until juices are bubbling and slightly thickened. Season to taste with salt and pepper, and serve hot.

Note: The dish can be prepared up to 2 days in advance and refrigerated, tightly covered. Reheat it, covered, in a 350°F oven for 20 to 25 minutes, or until hot.

Variation:

✳ Substitute 4 to 6 (6-ounce) boneless pork chops for the chicken.

> Calvados is an apple brandy that is one of Normandy's culinary claims to fame. It's frequently bottled with a small apple in the bottom. Although it's expensive, it's well worth the money, even for cooking.

Country Captain

Country Captain is a chicken dish that dates back to Colonial times. Some food historians say it originated in Savannah, Georgia, a major port for the spice trade. Other sources say a British captain brought the curry-flavored dish flecked with dried currants back from India. Serve it with some rice and a tossed salad.

Makes 4 to 6 servings | Prep time: 20 minutes | Minimum cook time: 3¼ hours in a medium slow cooker

1 (3- to 4-pound) chicken, cut into serving pieces, or 6 chicken pieces of your choice

3 tablespoons unsalted butter

1 large onion, diced

3 garlic cloves, minced

1 red bell pepper, seeds and ribs removed, and diced

1 tablespoon curry powder

½ teaspoon ground ginger

¼ teaspoon freshly grated nutmeg

½ teaspoon dried thyme

⅔ cup dried currants

1 (14.5-ounce) can diced tomatoes, undrained

⅔ cup Chicken Stock (page 21) or purchased stock

½ cup dry sherry

1 tablespoon cornstarch

Salt and freshly ground black pepper to taste

1. Rinse chicken and pat dry with paper towels. Preheat the oven broiler, and line a broiler pan with heavy-duty aluminum foil. Broil chicken pieces for 3 minutes per side, or until browned.

2. Melt butter in a medium skillet over medium-high heat. Add onion, garlic, and red bell pepper. Cook, stirring frequently, for 3 minutes, or until onion is translucent and pepper begins to soften. Reduce the heat to low, and stir in curry powder, ginger, nutmeg, and thyme. Cook for 1 minute, stirring constantly. Scrape mixture into the slow cooker.

3. Add currants, tomatoes, stock, and sherry to the slow cooker, and stir well. Arrange chicken pieces in the slow cooker, skin side down. Cook on Low for 6 to 8 hours or on High for 3 to 4 hours, or until chicken is cooked through, tender, and no longer pink.

4. If cooking on Low, raise the heat to High. Mix cornstarch and 2 tablespoons cold water in a small cup. Stir mixture into the slow cooker, and cook for an additional 10 to 20 minutes, or until the liquid is bubbling and has slightly thickened. Season to taste with salt and pepper, and serve hot.

Note: The dish can be prepared up to 2 days in advance and refrigerated, tightly covered. Reheat it, covered, in a 350°F oven for 20 to 25 minutes, or until hot.

Variation:

✳ Substitute 1½ pounds boneless pork loin for the chicken.

Sherry and vermouth can be stored for months at room temperature after they're opened, but red and white wine soon turn to vinegar, even if refrigerated. You can preserve them for future use in either of two ways: either freeze them right out of the bottle or reduce them and then freeze them. Freezing right out of the bottle is a great way to use them for marinades later on.

Chicken with Spring Vegetables

Chicken is inherently delicate, and that quality is conveyed beautifully in this light dish with accents of pearl onion, peas, and braised lettuce. Baked tomatoes and steamed potatoes are good partners for it on a plate.

Makes 4 to 6 servings | Prep time: 20 minutes | Minimum cook time: 3 1/4 hours in a medium slow cooker

1 (3- to 4-pound) chicken, cut into serving pieces, or 6 chicken pieces of your choice

2 cups Chicken Stock (page 21) or purchased stock

3 tablespoons chopped fresh parsley

1 tablespoon fresh thyme or 1/2 teaspoon dried

1 tablespoon fresh chopped rosemary or 1 teaspoon dried

1 tablespoon fresh tarragon or 1 teaspoon dried

1 bay leaf

2 garlic cloves, minced

1 (10-ounce) package frozen pearl onions, thawed

1 (10-ounce) package frozen peas, thawed

2 heads Bibb lettuce, trimmed, and cut into quarters

Salt and freshly ground black pepper to taste

1. Rinse chicken and pat dry with paper towels. Preheat the oven broiler, and line a broiler pan with heavy-duty aluminum foil. Broil chicken pieces for 3 minutes per side, or until browned.

2. Add stock, parsley, thyme, rosemary, tarragon, bay leaf, garlic, and pearl onions to the slow cooker, and stir well. Arrange chicken pieces in the slow cooker, skin side down. Cook on Low for 5 to 7 hours or on High for 2 1/2 to 3 hours, or until chicken is almost cooked through.

3. If cooking on Low, raise the heat to High. Add peas and lettuce, and cook for 45 to 55 minutes, or until lettuce is wilted, chicken is tender, and mixture is bubbling. Remove and discard bay leaf, season to taste with salt and pepper, and serve hot.

Note: The dish can be prepared up to 2 days in advance and refrigerated, tightly covered. Reheat it, covered, in a 350°F oven for 20 to 25 minutes, or until hot.

Indian Chicken with Toasted Cashews

In much of traditional Indian cooking chicken is marinated before being cooked, and the marinade becomes part of the sauce, thickened with pureed nuts to make it gluten-free. Aromatic basmati rice and some stewed lentils would create an authentic as well as delicious plate.

Makes 4 to 6 servings | Prep time: 15 minutes | Minimum cook time: 3 hours in a medium slow cooker

1 (6-ounce) container plain yogurt

4 garlic cloves, minced

2 tablespoons grated fresh ginger

2 tablespoons curry powder

½ teaspoon ground cinnamon

¼ to ½ teaspoon cayenne

Salt and freshly ground black pepper to taste

1 (3½ – 4-pound) frying chicken, cut into serving pieces, or 6 chicken pieces of your choice

1 cup roasted cashew nuts, divided

1½ cups Chicken Stock (page 21) or purchased stock

3 tablespoons vegetable oil

1 large onion, diced

1 carrot, sliced

1. Combine yogurt, garlic, ginger, curry powder, cinnamon, cayenne, salt, and pepper in heavy resealable plastic bag, and mix well. Rinse chicken and pat dry with paper towels. Add chicken pieces, and turn the bag to coat pieces evenly. Marinate chicken, refrigerated, for a minimum of 6 hours, preferably overnight.

2. Preheat the oven broiler, and line a broiler pan with heavy-duty aluminum foil. Remove chicken from marinade, scrape off marinade, and reserve marinade. Broil chicken pieces for 3 minutes per side, or until browned.

3. Grind ³/₄ cup cashews with ¹/₂ cup stock in a food processor fitted with a steel blade or in a blender. Set aside. Coarsely chop remaining cashews, and set aside.

4. Heat oil in large skillet over medium-high heat. Add onion, and cook, stirring frequently, for 3 minutes, or until onion is translucent. Add carrot to pan, along with nut puree, remaining chicken stock, and reserved marinade, and bring to a boil. Pour mixture into the slow cooker.

5. Arrange chicken pieces in the slow cooker, skin side down. Cook on Low for 6 to 8 hours or on High for 3 to 4 hours, or until chicken is cooked through, tender, and no longer pink. Season to taste with salt and pepper, and serve hot, sprinkled with remaining cashews.

Note: The dish can be prepared up to 2 days in advance and refrigerated, tightly covered. Reheat it, covered, in a 350°F oven for 20 to 25 minutes, or until hot.

Variation:

* Substitute 1¹/₂ pounds of stewing beef, cut into 1-inch cubes, for the chicken pieces. Add 2 hours if cooking on Low or 1 hour if cooking on High.

Acidophilus, an ingredient used to thicken yogurt, is a friendly bacteria, called a "probiotic" in some natural food circles. It lives in the intestines and helps prevent intestinal infections. Taking antibiotics can disturb the body's balance of friendly bacteria, which is why eating yogurt when taking antibiotics is frequently recommended.

Mexican Chicken and Rice (*Arroz con Pollo*)

Arroz con pollo is a fantastic one-dish meal. The rice is added midway through the cooking so it is perfectly cooked and not mushy. Olives and peas add visual interest along with their flavors.

Makes 4 to 6 servings | *Prep time: 20 minutes* | *Minimum cook time: 3 1/2 hours in a medium slow cooker*

1 (3- to 4-pound) chicken, cut into serving pieces, or 6 chicken pieces of your choice

1/3 cup olive oil, divided

1 large onion, diced

4 garlic cloves, minced

1/2 red bell pepper, seeds and ribs removed, and diced

1 tablespoon paprika

1 tablespoon chili powder

1 tablespoon ground cumin

2 teaspoons dried oregano

1 (14.5-ounce) can diced tomatoes, undrained

1/2 cup dry white wine

1/2 cup Chicken Stock (page 21) or purchased stock

1 bay leaf

1 cup uncooked converted long-grain rice

1/2 cup sliced pimiento-stuffed green olives

1 cup fresh peas or frozen peas, thawed

Salt and freshly ground black pepper to taste

1. Rinse chicken and pat dry with paper towels. Preheat the oven broiler, and line a broiler pan with heavy-duty aluminum foil. Broil chicken pieces for 3 minutes per side, or until browned.

2. Heat 2 tablespoons oil in a medium skillet over medium-high heat. Add onion, garlic, and bell pepper. Cook, stirring frequently, for 3 minutes, or until onion is translucent. Reduce the heat to low, and stir in paprika, chili powder, cumin, and oregano. Cook for 1 minute, stirring constantly. Scrape mixture into the slow cooker.

3. Add tomatoes, wine, stock, and bay leaf to the slow cooker, and stir well. Cook on Low for 4 to 6 hours or on High for 2 to 3 hours, or until chicken is almost cooked through.

4. While chicken cooks, add remaining oil to the skillet. Cook rice for 3 to 4 minutes, stirring frequently, or until grains are opaque and lightly browned. Remove the pan from the heat, and set aside.

5. If cooking on Low, raise the heat to High. Add rice to the slow cooker. Cook for 1 hour or until rice is almost tender and chicken is tender. Add olives and peas to the slow cooker. Cook for 10 to 15 minutes, or until peas are cooked.

Remove and discard bay leaf, season to taste with salt and pepper, and serve hot.

Note: The dish can be prepared up to 2 days in advance and refrigerated, tightly covered. Reheat it, covered, in a 350°F oven for 20 to 25 minutes, or until hot.

Variation:

✳ Add 1/4 pound sliced Spanish chorizo to the slow cooker along with the chicken.

It's important for the success of this dish and other dishes that include rice that you use long-grain converted rice such as Uncle Ben's. A shorter-grain rice will turn to mush. Converted white rice has undergone a steam-pressure process that makes the grains fluffier and keep separate when cooked.

Turkey Molé

This dark and thick sauce is made with a combination of spices, unsweetened cocoa powder, and thickened with peanut butter. It has a depth of flavor that's incredible, and the stew should be served over rice. A tossed salad is a good way to finish out the meal.

Makes 4 to 6 servings | Prep time: 20 minutes | Minimum cook time: 2 1/4 hours in a medium slow cooker

1 (1½-pound) boneless skinless turkey breast

2 tablespoons olive oil

2 large onions, diced

3 garlic cloves, minced

2 tablespoons chili powder

2 tablespoons unsweetened cocoa powder

2 teaspoons ground cumin

1 teaspoon ground coriander

¼ teaspoon ground cinnamon

1 (14.5-ounce) can diced tomatoes, drained

1½ cups Chicken Stock (page 21) or purchased stock

3 tablespoons smooth peanut butter

1 chipotle chile in adobo sauce, finely chopped

2 teaspoons adobo sauce

1 tablespoon cornstarch

Salt and freshly ground black pepper to taste

1. Rinse turkey and pat dry with paper towels. Trim fat, and cut turkey into 1-inch cubes.

2. Heat oil in a skillet over medium-high heat. Add onions and garlic, and cook, stirring frequently, for 3 minutes, or until onions are translucent. Reduce the heat to low, and stir in chili powder, cocoa powder, cumin, coriander, and cinnamon. Cook for 1 minute, stirring constantly. Scrape mixture into the slow cooker.

3. Add turkey, tomatoes, stock, peanut butter, chipotle chile, and adobo sauce to the slow cooker, and stir well. Cook on Low for 4 to 6 hours or on High for 2 to 3 hours, or until turkey is cooked through and no longer pink.

4. If cooking on Low, raise the heat to High. Mix cornstarch and 2 tablespoons cold water in a small cup, and stir it into the slow cooker. Cook for 15 to 20 minutes, or until juices are bubbling and slightly thickened. Season to taste with salt and pepper, and serve hot.

Note: The dish can be prepared up to 2 days in advance and refrigerated, tightly covered. Reheat it, covered, over low heat until hot, stirring occasionally.

Variation:

❋ Substitute 1½ pounds boneless pork loin, cut into 1-inch cubes, for the chicken.

> Mole is a thick and rich sauce made with unsweetened chocolate that dates back to the Aztec empire in Mexico. Legend states that King Montezuma, thinking that Cortez was a god, served mole at a banquet to receive him. The word mole comes from the Nahuatl word "milli," which means sauce or "concoction."

Creamy Chicken Stew with Wild Mushrooms

Woodsy wild mushrooms along with traditional stew vegetables such as carrots and celery enliven this dish finished with just enough cream to add richness. Serve it with some rice or Kasha (page 205) and a green vegetable.

Makes 4 to 6 servings | Prep time: 15 minutes | Minimum cook time: 2 1/4 hours in a medium slow cooker

1½ pounds boneless, skinless chicken (breast, thighs, or a combination)

¾ pound fresh shiitake mushrooms

2 tablespoons unsalted butter

2 tablespoons vegetable oil

1 onion, chopped

3 garlic cloves, minced

2 carrots, thinly sliced

1 celery rib, sliced

1 cup Chicken Stock (page 21) or purchased stock

½ cup dry white wine

2 tablespoons chopped fresh parsley

1 tablespoon fresh thyme or ½ teaspoon dried

1 tablespoon cornstarch

½ cup heavy cream

Salt and freshly ground black pepper to taste

1. Rinse chicken and pat dry with paper towels. Trim fat, and cut chicken into 1-inch cubes. Wipe mushrooms with a damp paper towel, discard stems, and cut in half if large.

2. Heat butter and oil in a medium skillet over medium-high heat. Add onion and garlic, and cook, stirring frequently, for 2 minutes. Add mushrooms, and cook, stirring frequently, for 3 to 4 minutes, or until mushrooms begin to soften. Scrape mixture into the slow cooker.

3. Add chicken, carrots, celery, stock, wine, parsley, and thyme to the slow cooker, and stir well. Cook on Low for 4 to 6 hours or on High for 2 to 3 hours, or until chicken is cooked through and no longer pink and vegetables are tender.

4. If cooking on Low, raise the heat to High. Stir cornstarch into cream, and stir cream mixture into the slow cooker. Cook for an additional 15 to 20 minutes, or until juices are bubbling and slightly thickened. Season to taste with salt and pepper, and serve hot.

Note: The dish can be prepared up to 2 days in advance and refrigerated, tightly covered. Reheat it, covered, over low heat until hot, stirring occasionally.

Variation:

✳ Substitute boneless pork loin for the chicken. Brown the pork in a skillet.

> Heat and light are the two worst enemies of dried herbs and spices, so a pretty display rack over the stove is about the worst place to store them. Keep them in a cool, dark place to preserve their potency. The best test for freshness and potency is to smell the contents. If you don't smell a strong aroma, you need a new bottle.

Indonesian Chicken Curry

This form of curry became very popular in the Netherlands in the nineteenth century because they had substantial land holdings in the part of Southeast Asia that is now Indonesia. It is a fairly mild curry, and the coconut milk makes it appear creamy.

Makes 4 to 6 servings | Prep time: 20 minutes | Minimum cook time: 2¼ hours in a medium slow cooker

1½ pounds boneless, skinless chicken (breast, thighs, or a combination)

1 tablespoon Asian sesame oil

2 tablespoons grated fresh ginger

3 scallions, white parts and 4 inches of green tops, chopped

3 garlic cloves, minced

2 tablespoons curry powder or to taste

1 teaspoon ground cumin

1 carrot, sliced on the diagonal

½ red bell pepper, seeds and ribs removed, and cut into 1-inch squares

1 cup Chicken Stock (page 21) or purchased stock

1 cup canned unsweetened coconut milk

2 tablespoons rice wine vinegar

2 tablespoons firmly packed dark brown sugar

1 tablespoon soy sauce

1 cup sliced bok choy or Napa cabbage

2 ripe plum tomatoes, cored, seeded, and cut into sixths

1½ tablespoons cornstarch

Salt and freshly ground black pepper to taste

For serving: Chutney, raisins, thinly sliced scallions, sweetened coconut, slivered almonds

1. Rinse chicken and pat dry with paper towels. Trim fat, and cut chicken into 1-inch cubes.

2. Heat oil in a small skillet over medium-high heat. Add ginger, scallions, and garlic, and cook, stirring frequently, for 30 seconds, or until fragrant. Reduce the heat to low, and stir in curry powder and cumin. Cook for 1 minute, stirring constantly. Scrape mixture into the slow cooker.

3. Add chicken, carrot, red bell pepper, stock, coconut milk, vinegar, brown sugar, and soy sauce to the slow cooker, and stir well. Cook on Low for 3 to 5 hours or on High for 1½ to 2 hours, or until chicken is cooked through. Add bok choy and tomatoes, and cook for 1 more hour on Low or 30 minutes on High, or until bok choy is crisp-tender.

4. If cooking on Low, raise the heat to High. Mix cornstarch with 2 tablespoons cold water, and stir cornstarch mixture into the slow cooker. Cook for an additional 15 to 20 minutes, or until juices are bubbling and slightly thickened. Season to taste with salt and pepper, and serve hot, passing condiments separately.

Note: The dish can be prepared up to 2 days in advance and refrigerated, tightly covered. Reheat it, covered, over low heat until hot, stirring occasionally.

Variations:

* Substitute vegetable stock for the chicken stock and extra firm tofu for the chicken.
* Substitute 1½ pounds boneless pork loin, cut into 1-inch cubes, for the chicken.

Frequently coconut milk separates in the can with the liquid on the bottom and a thick layer of coconut on top. Whisk it briskly until the lumps are gone because they will not break up well with the low heat in the slow cooker.

Santa Fe Turkey Meatloaf

Meatloaf takes on a lusty Hispanic flavor in this version bound by cornmeal and given some crunch with crushed corn tortilla chips. Serve it with some Cowboy Beans (page 203) or Refried Beans (page 209).

Makes 4 to 6 servings | Prep time: 20 minutes | Minimum cook time: 2^1/$_2$ hours in a medium slow cooker

3 tablespoons olive oil

1 medium onion, chopped

½ red or green bell pepper, seeds and ribs removed, and chopped

3 garlic cloves, minced

2 jalapeño or serrano chiles, seeds and ribs removed, and finely chopped

2 tablespoons chili powder

2 teaspoons dried oregano

2 teaspoons ground cumin

2 large eggs, lightly beaten

¼ cup whole milk

¼ cup yellow cornmeal

¼ cup chopped fresh cilantro

1 chipotle chile in adobo sauce, finely chopped

¾ cup crushed corn tortilla chips

¾ cup grated smoked cheddar cheese

1½ pounds ground turkey

Salt and freshly ground black pepper to taste

1. Heat oil in a small skillet over medium-high heat. Add onion, bell pepper, garlic, and chile. Cook, stirring frequently, for 3 minutes, or until onion is translucent. Reduce the heat to low, and stir in chili powder, oregano, and cumin. Cook for 1 minute, stirring constantly. Set aside.

2. Combine eggs, milk, cornmeal, cilantro, chipotle chile, crushed tortilla chips, and cheese in a large mixing bowl, and stir well. Add turkey and vegetable mixture, and mix well.

3. Grease the inside of the slow cooker insert liberally with vegetable oil spray. Fold a sheet of heavy-duty aluminum foil in half, and place it in the bottom of the slow cooker with the sides of the foil extending up the sides of the slow cooker. Form turkey mixture into an oval or round, depending on the shape of your cooker, and place it into the cooker on top of the foil.

4. Cook meatloaf on Low for 5 to 6 hours or on High for 2^1/$_2$ to 3 hours, or until an instant-read thermometer inserted into the center of the loaf registers 165°F. Remove meatloaf from the slow cooker by pulling it up by the sides of the foil. Drain off any grease from the foil, and slide meatloaf onto a serving platter. Serve hot.

Note: The dish can be prepared up to 2 days in advance and refrigerated, tightly covered. Reheat it, covered, in a 350°F oven for 20 to 25 minutes, or until hot.

Variations:
* Substitute jalapeño Jack cheese for the smoked cheddar.
* Substitute ground beef and pork for the turkey; the cooking time will remain the same.
* Add ½ cup fresh corn kernels or frozen corn, thawed, to the turkey mixture.

If one of the reasons why you're using turkey rather than beef or another red meat is to cut back on cholesterol, another way to add a health benefit to this recipe is to substitute two egg whites for the one whole egg. While in baking it is difficult to make this substitution, the purpose of the egg in the meatloaf is to hold it together, so it's fine.

Spanish Chicken with Garbanzo Beans

The combination of aromatic smoked Spanish paprika and heady sherry are the two essential ingredients in this flavorful stew. While rice is always appropriate, I like to serve this with Kasha (page 205), which reinforces the nutty flavor of the beans.

Makes 4 to 6 servings | Prep time: 25 minutes | Minimum cook time: 3 1/2 hours in a medium slow cooker

1½ pounds boneless, skinless chicken (breast, thighs, or a combination)

2 tablespoons olive oil

1 large onion, diced

6 garlic cloves, minced, divided

1 large carrot, sliced

1 celery rib, sliced

3 tablespoons smoked Spanish paprika

1 tablespoon chili powder

2 teaspoons ground cumin

1 (14.5-ounce) can diced tomatoes, undrained

1 cup Chicken Stock (page 21) or purchased stock

½ cup dry sherry

2 tablespoons tomato paste

2 (15-ounce) cans garbanzo beans, drained and rinsed

1 bay leaf

¼ cup chopped fresh parsley

Salt and freshly ground black pepper to taste

1. Rinse chicken and pat dry with paper towels. Trim fat and cut chicken into 1-inch cubes.

2. Heat oil in a medium skillet over medium-high heat. Add onion, half of garlic, carrot, and celery. Cook, stirring frequently, for 3 minutes, or until onion is translucent. Reduce the heat to low, and stir in paprika, chili powder, and cumin. Cook for 1 minute, stirring constantly. Scrape mixture into the slow cooker.

3. Add chicken, tomatoes, stock, sherry, tomato paste, beans, and bay leaf to the slow cooker, and stir well. Cook on Low for 4 to 6 hours or on High for 2 to 3 hours, or until chicken is cooked through and no longer pink.

4. While chicken cooks, combine parsley and remaining garlic in a small bowl, and set aside. Remove and discard bay leaf, season to taste with salt and pepper, and serve hot, sprinkled with parsley mixture.

Note: The dish can be prepared up to 2 days in advance and refrigerated, tightly covered. Reheat it, covered, over low heat until hot, stirring occasionally.

Variation:
* Substitute 1½ pounds boneless pork loin, cut into 1-inch cubes, for the chicken.

Sherry is a brandy-fortified wine made from white Palomino grapes grown near the town of Jerez in southern Spain. Sherry is the Anglicization of *Jerez*, and authentic sherry comes in a range of styles from bone dry to very sweet.

Turkey Chili

Turkey chili now vies in popularity with beef chili. However, the recipes need to be formulated differently to showcase the best attributes of both meats. In this version a bit of dark brown sugar and a smoky chipotle chile do just that.

Makes 4 to 6 servings | Prep time: 15 minutes | Minimum cook time: 2 hours in a medium slow cooker

3 tablespoons olive oil

1 large onion, chopped

1 red or green bell pepper, seeds and ribs removed, and chopped

3 garlic cloves, minced

1 jalapeño or serrano chile, seeds and ribs removed, and finely chopped

3 tablespoons chili powder

2 tablespoons ground cumin

1 tablespoon smoked Spanish paprika

2 teaspoons dried oregano

1½ pounds ground turkey

2 (14.5-ounce) cans diced tomatoes, undrained

1 (8-ounce) can tomato sauce

1 tablespoon firmly packed dark brown sugar

1 chipotle chile in adobo sauce, finely chopped

2 (15-ounce) cans red kidney beans, drained and rinsed

Salt and freshly ground black pepper to taste

Fresh cilantro leaves

1. Heat oil in a large skillet over medium-high heat. Add onion, bell pepper, garlic, and chile. Cook, stirring frequently, for 3 minutes, or until onion is translucent. Reduce the heat to low, and stir in chili powder, cumin, paprika, and oregano. Cook for 1 minute, stirring constantly. Scrape mixture into the slow cooker.

2. Add turkey, tomatoes, tomato sauce, brown sugar, chipotle chile, and beans to the slow cooker, and stir well. Cook on Low for 4 to 6 hours or on High for 2 to 3 hours, or until vegetables are soft. Season to taste with salt and pepper, and serve hot, sprinkling each serving with cilantro leaves.

Note: The dish can be prepared up to 2 days in advance and refrigerated, tightly covered. Reheat it, covered, over low heat until hot, stirring occasionally.

Variation:

✳ Substitute ground veal or a mixture of ground veal and ground pork for the turkey. Add 1 hour if cooking on Low or 30 minutes if cooking on High.

A can of chipotle chiles in adobo sauce goes a long way. Chances are you use only one or two chiles in a given recipe. To save the remainder of the can, place a few chilies with a teaspoon of sauce in ice cube trays. When they're frozen, transfer them to a heavy resealable plastic bag. Be sure to wash the ice cube tray well.

Cajun Turkey Meatloaf

The part of meatloaf that excludes it from a gluten-free diet is the inclusion of some sort of breadcrumbs made from wheat bread in the meat mixture. Oats perform the same function in this version, and cooking meatloaf in the moist heat of the slow cooker keeps it from drying out.

Makes 4 to 6 servings | Prep time: 20 minutes | Minimum cook time: 2 1/2 hours in a medium slow cooker

2 tablespoons olive oil

1 medium onion, chopped

1 small carrot, chopped

1 celery rib, chopped

2 garlic cloves, minced

2 large eggs, lightly beaten

1/4 cup whole milk

1/2 cup gluten-free quick oats

1/2 cup grated sharp cheddar

3 tablespoons chopped fresh parsley

1 tablespoon Cajun seasoning

1/2 teaspoon dried thyme

Freshly ground black pepper to taste

1 1/2 pounds ground turkey

1/2 cup bottled chili sauce

2 tablespoons cider vinegar

2 tablespoons firmly packed dark brown sugar

Vegetable oil spray

1. Heat oil in a small skillet over medium-high heat. Add onion, carrot, celery, and garlic, and cook, stirring frequently, for 3 minutes, or until onion is translucent. Set aside.

2. Combine eggs, milk, oats, cheese, parsley, Cajun seasoning, thyme, and pepper in a large mixing bowl, and stir well. Add turkey and vegetable mixture, and mix well. Combine chili sauce, vinegar, and brown sugar in a small bowl, and stir well.

3. Grease the inside of the slow cooker insert liberally with vegetable oil spray. Fold a sheet of heavy-duty aluminum foil in half, and place it in the bottom of the slow cooker with the sides of the foil extending up the sides of the slow cooker. Form turkey mixture into an oval or round, depending on the shape of your cooker, and place it into the cooker on top of the foil. Spread chili sauce mixture on top of turkey.

4. Cook meatloaf on Low for 5 to 6 hours or on High for 2 1/2 to 3 hours, or until an instant-read thermometer inserted into the center of the loaf registers 165°F. Remove meatloaf from the slow cooker by pulling it up by the sides of the foil. Drain off any grease from the foil, and slide meatloaf onto a serving platter. Serve hot.

Note: The dish can be prepared up to 2 days in advance and refrigerated, tightly covered. Reheat it, covered, in a 350°F oven for 20 to 25 minutes, or until hot.

Variations:

* Substitute ground beef and pork for the turkey; the cooking time will remain the same.

* Place a row of hard-cooked eggs in the center of the meatloaf before cooking.

* Add 1/2 pound diced sautéed mushrooms.

* Add 1 cup frozen chopped spinach, thawed and squeezed dry.

* Substitute 2 teaspoons Italian seasoning plus salt to taste for the Cajun seasoning salt, and substitute whole milk mozzarella for the cheddar cheese.

Oats are naturally gluten-free, however many brands suffer from cross contamination from wheat, either in the field or in processing plants. Certain companies have taken meticulous pains to be allowed to market their product as gluten-free. Look for that on the bag.

Sweet and Sour Stuffed Cabbage

This dish is drawn from Eastern Europe, where cabbage was a popular vegetable during all the winter months. Because there's rice in the turkey mixture, it becomes a one-dish dinner too.

Makes 4 to 6 servings | Prep time: 25 minutes | Minimum cook time: 4 hours in a medium slow cooker

1 small head (about 1½ pounds) green cabbage

1½ pounds ground turkey

1 cup cooked white or brown rice

1 small onion, grated

Salt and freshly ground black pepper to taste

2 McIntosh or Rome apples, peeled, cored, and diced

½ cup raisins

1 (8-ounce) can tomato sauce

½ cup cider vinegar

½ cup firmly packed dark brown sugar

1. Bring a 4-quart saucepan of water to a boil. Remove core from cabbage by cutting around it with a sharp knife. Pull off 10 to 12 large leaves from outside and set aside. Cut remaining cabbage in half, and cut off 2 cups thin shreds. Blanch leaves and shreds in the boiling water for 5 minutes and then drain.

2. Combine ground turkey, rice, onion, salt, and pepper in a mixing bowl. Mix well.

3. Place half of drained cabbage shreds into the bottom of the slow cooker. Top with half of apples and half of raisins. Place ¹/₂ cup turkey mixture at the root end of a cabbage leaf. Tuck in sides, and roll up leaf into a cylinder. Repeat with remaining cabbage leaves and turkey filling. Place rolls seam side down in the slow cooker in a single layer. Top with remaining cabbage shreds, apple, and raisins, and start a new layer of cabbage rolls, if necessary.

4. Mix tomato sauce, vinegar, and brown sugar in a mixing bowl. Stir well to dissolve sugar. Pour sauce over cabbage rolls. Cook on Low for 8 to 10 hours or on High for 4 to 5 hours, or until the sauce is bubbly and an instant-read thermometer inserted into turkey filling reads 165°F.

Note: The dish can be prepared up to 2 days in advance and refrigerated, tightly covered. Reheat it, covered, in a 350°F oven for 20 to 25 minutes, or until hot.

Variation:

✱ Substitute ground beef for the ground turkey. The cooking time will not change.

If it matters how the apples in the dish look, then peeling, coring, and then slicing each half or quarter is still the best method. But if the apples are going to be hidden as in this dish, there's a faster way: Peel the apple and keep turning it in your hand as you cut off slices. Soon all you'll be left with is the core, which you can discard. It's much faster.

Mexican Chicken Stew

In addition to serving this flavorful stew as a distinct dish, you can also use it as the base for a tamale pie, using Fontina Polenta (page 197) as the topping. It contains canned beans, so the cooking time is relatively short.

Makes 4 to 6 servings | Prep time: 15 minutes | Minimum cook time: 2 1/2 hours in a medium slow cooker

1½ pounds boneless, skinless chicken (breast, thighs, or a combination)

3 tablespoons olive oil

1 large onion, diced

3 garlic cloves, minced

1 red bell pepper, seeds and ribs removed, and diced

1 jalapeño or serrano chile, seeds and ribs removed, and finely chopped

2 tablespoons chili powder

2 teaspoons ground cumin

1 teaspoon dried oregano

1 cup refrigerated commercial tomato salsa

¾ cup Chicken Stock (page 21) or purchased stock

1 (8-ounce) can tomato sauce

1 (15-ounce) can pinto beans, drained and rinsed

Salt and freshly ground black pepper to taste

1. Rinse chicken and pat dry with paper towels. Trim fat, and cut chicken into 1-inch cubes.

2. Heat oil in a medium skillet over medium-high heat. Add onion, garlic, bell pepper, and chile. Cook, stirring frequently, for 3 minutes, or until onion is translucent. Reduce the heat to low, and stir in chili powder, cumin, and oregano. Cook for 1 minute, stirring constantly. Scrape mixture into the slow cooker.

3. Add chicken, salsa, stock, tomato sauce, and beans to the slow cooker, and stir well. Cook on Low for 4 to 6 hours or on High for 2 to 3 hours, or until chicken is cooked through, tender, and no longer pink. Season to taste with salt and pepper, and serve hot.

Note: The dish can be prepared up to 2 days in advance and refrigerated, tightly covered. Reheat it, covered, over low heat until hot, stirring occasionally.

Variation:

✳ Substitute 1½ pounds boneless pork loin, cut into 1-inch cubes, for the chicken.

Be careful when cooking hot chilies that the steam from the pan doesn't get in your eyes. The potent oils in the peppers can be transmitted in the vapor.

Chapter 7

From the Pastures and Prairies:

Meat Stews and Braises

*I*f you were like me, and almost everyone I know, then the first dish you cooked in a slow cooker was a pot roast or beef stew. Tenderizing inexpensive cuts of beef was touted as the miracle use of this simple appliance, and indeed the perception is correct. The slow cooker is an appliance that braises, and that's what these dishes need.

No cuisine or culture can claim braising, although we've borrowed our English word from the French. While they may be called sand pots in China, ragouts in France and stews in North America, every culture has less tender cuts of meat, that are usually also less expensive, that are simmered in aromatic liquid for many hours until they're tender.

That's what braising is all about—tenderness. And the amount of time it takes to reach the descriptive state of "fork tender" depends on each individual piece of meat; there are no hard and fast rules. That's why soups can take almost as long to cook as stews, and stews can take almost as long to cook as whole roasts.

Braising is a low heat method, since the meat is the same temperature as the simmering liquid, 212°F. This simmering converts the collagen of the meat's connective tissue to gelatin, so the meat is tender.

If possible, it's best to cook them in advance and chill them. That way all the saturated fat rises to the top and becomes a hard layer once the food chills. It can then be removed in its entirety, and very easily at that. An alternative to removing the fat, if you're serving the dish the same day, is to tilt the slow cooker insert by setting one side about 2 inches higher than the other. That way the fat will create a pool on the low side, and it can be ladled off with a soup ladle.

Choosing the Choicest

The best beef, in terms of both flavor and texture, comes from cows 18 to 24 months old. Beef is graded in the U.S. by the Department of Agriculture as Prime, Choice, or Select. Prime is usually reserved for restaurants, and the other two are what is found in supermarkets. Since the age, color, texture, and marbling is what determines its category, Prime beef is the most marbled and contains the most fat.

When you're looking at beef in the case, seek deep red, moist meat generously marbled with white fat. Yellow fat is a tip-off to old age. Beef is purple after cutting but the meat quickly "blooms" to bright red on exposure to the air. Well-aged beef is dark and dry. To avoid paying for waste, be sure meat is thoroughly trimmed by a butcher. Otherwise a low per pound price can translate into a higher cost for the edible portion.

You can usually save money by cutting the meat into cubes yourself, and then you have the bones in the freezer to make Beef Stock (page 23). The general guideline is that if it's less expensive, then it's the cut you want. But here are some specifics:

* Chuck is the beef taken from between the neck and shoulder blades. Some chuck roasts also contain a piece of the blade bone, but it's easy to cull the meat from a chuck roast.
* Round is the general name for the large quantity of beef from the hind leg extending from the rump to the ankle. The eye of the round and the bottom round are the two least tender cuts, while the top round should be reserved for roasting.

The Benefits of Browning

For red meats like beef, veal, or lamb, browning is the initial step to a delicious dish; it's an optional step for poultry and pork, and totally unnecessary for fish and seafood. What browning accomplishes is actually giving the foods better flavor.

It's called the Maillard Reaction, and it was named for an early twentieth century chemist, Louis Camille Maillard, who discovered it. It's a chemical reaction that takes place on the surface of meats that creates the development of flavor. The reaction takes place when food reaches 285°F, and that can only be done in a hot pan before food is cooked. Otherwise the temperature of the meat only reaches 212°F, which is the simmering temperature of the braising liquid.

Browning seals in juices as it makes foods more visually appealing, too. Here are some tips for browning foods to be braised:

* **Dry food well.** Moisture causes splatters, which messes up the stove, and can burn the cook.
* **Preheat the broiler well if using that method.** For gluten-free cooking, all meats can be browned under the under the broiler as well as in a skillet. (If cooking with wheat flour the flour needs the fat in a skillet to brown it correctly.) But you want to preheat the broiler for at least 10 or 15 minutes to create the brown crust.
* **Preheat the pan if using that method.** You have to wait until the fat is very hot, or the food will not brown.
* **Don't crowd the pan.** For food to brown it needs room for the steam to escape that's created when the cold food hits the hot pan.

Boeuf Bourguignon

This dish with cubes of tender beef blended with onions and mushrooms in a red wine sauce is a classic of Burgundy. Serve it with some steamed new potatoes to enjoy all the flavorful sauce, and a steamed green vegetable such as string beans.

Makes 6 to 8 servings | Active time: 25 minutes | Minimum cook time: 4 hours in a medium slow cooker

2 pounds stewing beef, fat trimmed, and cut into 1-inch cubes

2 tablespoons olive oil

1 large onion, diced

3 garlic cloves, minced

½ pound white mushrooms, rinsed, stemmed, and sliced

2 cups dry red wine

½ cup Beef Stock (page 23) or purchased stock

1 tablespoon tomato paste

3 tablespoons chopped fresh parsley

1 teaspoon herbes de Provence or dried thyme

1 bay leaf

1½ tablespoons cornstarch

Salt and freshly ground black pepper to taste

1. Preheat the oven broiler, and line a broiler pan with heavy-duty aluminum foil. Broil beef for 3 minutes per side, or until browned. Transfer beef to the slow cooker, and pour in any juices that have collected in the pan.

2. Heat oil in a medium skillet over medium heat. Add onion, garlic, and mushrooms. Cook, stirring frequently, for 4 to 5 minutes, or until onion is translucent and mushrooms are soft. Scrape mixture into the slow cooker.

3. Add wine, stock, tomato paste, parsley, herbes de Provence, and bay leaf to the slow cooker, and stir well. Cook on Low for 8 to 10 hours or on High for 4 to 5 hours, or until beef is tender.

4. If cooking on Low, raise the heat to High. Mix cornstarch and 2 tablespoons cold water in a small cup, and stir cornstarch mixture into the slow cooker. Cook for an additional 15 to 20 minutes, or until juices are bubbling and slightly thickened. Remove and discard bay leaf, season to taste with salt and pepper, and serve hot.

Note: The dish can be prepared up to 2 days in advance and refrigerated, tightly covered. Reheat it, covered, in a 350°F oven for 20 to 25 minutes, or until hot.

Variation:

✳ Substitute boneless lamb shoulder for the beef, and add 2 tablespoons chopped fresh rosemary or 2 teaspoons dried to the recipe.

I have a great use for the leftover red wine; I drink it. If you don't want to drink it, here's what to do: Boil it down in a saucepan until it's reduced by half, then freeze it in ice cube trays. When you're making a dish in the future that calls for red wine, just pull out a few cubes.

Picadillo

While flavored like a traditional chili, the addition of cinnamon and raisins gives this authentic Mexican dish a distinctive character. Serve it over some brown or white rice with a tossed salad on the side.

Makes 4 to 6 servings | Active time: 15 minutes | Minimum cook time: 3 hours in a medium slow cooker

3 tablespoons olive oil, divided

1½ pounds ground beef

1 large onion, diced

3 garlic cloves, minced

1 jalapeño or serrano chile, seeds and ribs removed, finely chopped

2 tablespoons chili powder

1 teaspoon ground cumin

½ teaspoon ground cinnamon

1 (14.5-ounce) can diced tomatoes, undrained

½ cup Beef Stock (page 23) or purchased stock

1 (4-ounce) can diced mild green chiles, drained

2 tablespoons cider vinegar

½ cup raisins

Salt and cayenne to taste

1. Heat 1 tablespoon oil in a skillet over medium-high heat. Crumble ground beef into the skillet, and cook for 2 minutes to brown well on the bottom. Mash beef with a potato masher, and cook for an additional 2 to 3 minutes, or until browned. Remove beef from the pan with a slotted spoon, and transfer it to the slow cooker. Discard grease from the skillet.

2. Heat remaining oil in a skillet over medium-high heat. Add onion, garlic, and chile. Cook, stirring frequently, for 3 minutes, or until onion is translucent. Reduce the heat to low, and stir in chili powder, cumin, and cinnamon. Cook for 1 minute, stirring constantly. Scrape mixture into the slow cooker.

3. Add tomatoes, stock, green chilies, vinegar, and raisins to the slow cooker, and stir well. Cook on Low for 6 to 8 hours or on High for 3 to 4 hours, or until beef is tender. Season to taste with salt and cayenne, and serve hot.

Note: The dish can be prepared up to 2 days in advance and refrigerated, tightly covered. Reheat it, covered, over low heat until hot, stirring occasionally.

Variations:

✳ Substitute ground turkey for the ground beef.

✳ Substitute chopped dried apricots or dried cranberries for the raisins.

> Any chili can become a finger food by turning it into nachos. Pile the chili on large nacho corn chips, top with some grated Monterey Jack cheese, and pop them under the broiler until the cheese is melted.

Barbecued Smoked Pork

Searing meats over aromatic woods on the grill, and then giving them time in the slow cooker, you can replicate the wonderful heady flavor and falling apart tenderness of traditional barbecue.

Makes 6 to 8 servings | Active time: 20 minutes | Minimum cook time: 4 hours in a medium slow cooker

1½ cups hickory or mesquite chips

1 (2½-pound) boneless pork shoulder

2 garlic cloves, crushed

Salt and freshly ground black pepper to taste

1½ cups Chicken Stock (page 21) or purchased stock

Salt and freshly ground black pepper to taste

1 cup Gingered Barbecue Sauce (page 221) or commercial gluten-free barbecue sauce

1. If using a charcoal grill, soak the chips in water for at least 30 minutes. If using a gas grill, place the dry chips in a 12x18-inch piece of heavy-duty aluminum foil. Bring up the foil on all sides, and roll the ends together to seal the packet. Poke several small holes in the top of the packet.

2. Rub pork with garlic, salt, and pepper. Drain the wood chips, and sprinkle chips on the hot coals, or place packet over preheated grid. Place pork on the grill rack and close the grill's lid, or cover it with a sheet of heavy heavy-duty aluminum foil. Smoke pork for 10 minutes per side, turning it with tongs.

3. Place pork in the slow cooker and add stock. Cook pork for 8 to 10 hours on Low or 4 to 5 hours on High, or until meat is very tender. Season to taste with salt and pepper.

4. Remove pork from the slow cooker, and slice it against the grain into thin slices. Spoon some pan juices over meat, and pass barbecue sauce separately.

Note: The dish can be prepared up to 2 days in advance and refrigerated, tightly covered. Reheat it, covered, in a 350°F oven for 20 to 25 minutes, or until hot.

Variation:

✳ Substitute beef brisket for the pork shoulder, and substitute beef stock for the chicken stock. Increase the cooking time by 2 hours on Low or 1 hour on High.

Most people on gluten-free diets know that they have to spend time examining all processed foods looking for lurking gluten. One category of these foods, unfortunately, is barbecue sauce. Many are thickened with wheat proteins.

New England Boiled Dinner

This is a more flavorful version of classic corned beef and cabbage because it cooks in chicken stock and wine rather than water. There's not enough room in the slow cooker for everything, so make some steamed potatoes to serve on the side.

Makes 6 to 8 servings | *Active time: 15 minutes* | *Minimum cook time: 5 hours in a medium slow cooker*

1 (2- to 2½-pound) corned beef brisket

1 onion, thickly sliced

2 celery ribs, thickly sliced

2 carrots, thickly sliced

2 garlic cloves, minced

1 bay leaf

½ small green cabbage

2 cups Chicken Stock (page 21) or purchased stock

1 cup dry white wine

Freshly ground black pepper to taste

Dijon mustard for serving

1. Cut off as much fat as possible from top of corned beef. Rinse and set aside. Place onion, celery, carrot, garlic, and bay leaf in the slow cooker. Place corned beef on top of vegetables.

2. Cut cabbage in half. Cut core from one half, and slice into wedges. Arrange wedges on top of corned beef. Pour stock and wine into the slow cooker.

3. Cook on Low for 10 to 12 hours or on High for 5 to 6 hours, or until corned beef is tender. Remove as much grease as possible from the slow cooker with a soup ladle.

4. Remove and discard bay leaf, and thinly slice corned beef against the grain. Serve it with cabbage and other vegetables. Pass mustard separately.

Note: The dish can be prepared up to 2 days in advance and refrigerated, tightly covered. Reheat it, covered, in a 350°F oven for 20 to 25 minutes, or until hot.

Variations:

✳ Substitute parsnips or turnips for the carrot.

✳ Substitute water for the mixture of stock and wine.

You'll see two types of corned beef in the market, the blade cut and the flat cut. Both are forms of beef brisket, but the thicker blade cut contains a lot more fat, and that's why it sells for a much cheaper price. You're better off with the flat cut because the shrinkage is much less and the proportion of edible meat is higher.

Real Chili Con Carne

Real chili con carne is just that, meat cooked in a sauce laced with chiles. And no Texan would make it with ground beef; it's always made with small cubes of chuck or another cut of meat for braising. But like all chili, serve it over rice and pass the garnishes too.

Makes 4 to 6 servings | *Active time: 20 minutes* | *Minimum cook time: 3 hours in a medium slow cooker*

1½ pounds stewing beef, fat trimmed, and cut into ½-inch cubes

2 tablespoons vegetable oil

1 large onion, diced

4 garlic cloves, minced

1 jalapeño or serrano chile, seeds and ribs removed, and finely chopped

½ green bell pepper, seeds and ribs removed, and finely chopped

3 tablespoons chili powder

1 tablespoon smoked Spanish paprika

1 tablespoon ground cumin

1 teaspoon dried oregano

1 (8-ounce) can tomato sauce

2 (14.5-ounce) cans diced tomatoes, drained

1 chipotle chile in adobo sauce, finely chopped

2 teaspoons adobo sauce

1 (15-ounce) can red kidney beans, drained and rinsed

1 cup corn kernels

Salt and freshly ground black pepper to taste

For serving: sour cream, chopped onion, grated Monterey Jack cheese

1. Preheat the oven broiler, and line a broiler pan with heavy-duty aluminum foil. Broil beef for 3 minutes per side, or until browned. Transfer beef to the slow cooker, and pour in any juices that have collected in the pan.

2. Heat oil in a medium skillet over medium-high heat. Add onion, garlic, chile, and green bell pepper. Cook, stirring frequently, for 3 minutes, or until onion is translucent. Reduce the heat to low, and stir in chili powder, paprika, cumin, and oregano. Cook for 1 minute, stirring constantly. Scrape mixture into the slow cooker.

3. Add tomato sauce, tomatoes, chipotle chile, and adobo sauce to the slow cooker, and stir well. Cook on Low for 4 to 6 hours or on High for 2 to 3 hours. Add beans and corn, and cook for an additional 2 hours on Low or 1 hour on High, or until beef is very tender. Season to taste with salt and pepper, and serve hot.

4. When serving, pass sour cream, onion, and cheese separately.

Note: The dish can be prepared up to 2 days in advance and refrigerated, tightly covered. Reheat it, covered, over low heat until hot, stirring occasionally.

Variation:

✳ Substitute cubes of turkey for the beef. It is not necessary to do any pre-browning, and reduce the cooking time by 2 hours on Low and 1 hour on High.

The city of San Antonio, Texas, claims to be the birthplace of American chili con carne. Back in the 1880s brightly dressed "chili queens" sold bowls of chili from cars located around the city's Military Plaza, and in 1893 the San Antonio Chili Stand at the Columbian Exposition in Chicago introduced the dish to other parts of the country. In 1977 the state of Texas proclaimed chili as the state's official dish.

Herbed Pot Roast

Oven-roasted or mashed potatoes are the best choices to go with this tender and flavorful roast. The vegetables are already in the slow cooker with it.

Makes 4 to 6 servings | Prep time: 15 minutes | Minimum cook time: 4 hours in a medium slow cooker

1 (2- to 2½-pound) boneless chuck roast or rump roast

3 tablespoons olive oil

1 large sweet onion, such as Vidalia or Bermuda, diced

3 garlic cloves, minced

2 cups Beef Stock (page 23) or purchased stock

4 celery ribs, trimmed and cut into 1-inch slices

2 carrots, cut into 1-inch lengths, and halved if thick

3 tablespoons chopped fresh rosemary or 1 tablespoon dried

2 tablespoons chopped fresh parsley

1 tablespoon chopped fresh thyme or ½ teaspoon dried

1½ tablespoons cornstarch

Salt and freshly ground black pepper to taste

1. Preheat the oven broiler, and line a broiler pan with heavy-duty aluminum foil. Broil beef for 3 to 4 minutes per side, or until browned. Transfer beef to the slow cooker, and pour in any juices that have collected in the pan.

2. Heat oil in a medium skillet over medium-high heat. Add onion and garlic, and cook, stirring frequently, for 3 minutes, or until onion is translucent. Scrape mixture into the slow cooker.

3. Add stock, celery, carrots, and rosemary to the slow cooker, and stir well. Cook on Low for 8 to 10 hours or on High for 4 to 5 hours, or until beef is very tender. Remove as much grease as possible from the slow cooker with a soup ladle.

4. If cooking on Low, raise the heat to High. Mix cornstarch with 2 tablespoons cold water in a small cup, and stir cornstarch mixture into the slow cooker. Cook on High for 15 to 20 minutes, or until juices are bubbling and slightly thickened. Season to taste with salt and pepper, and serve hot.

5. Remove beef from the slow cooker, and slice it against the grain into thin slices. Serve immediately.

Note: The dish can be prepared up to 2 days in advance and refrigerated, tightly covered. Reheat it, covered, in a 350°F oven for 20 to 25 minutes, or until hot.

While roasted meats need time to "rest" during which the juices are reabsorbed into the fibers of the meat, that is not necessary for braised dishes. The juices from the meat are integrated into the sauce, which then moistens the meat.

Spanish Lamb Shanks

The addition of a bit of citrus and smoked paprika contrasted with woodsy dried mushrooms, fresh herbs, and caramelized onions bring out all the luscious fruit in the wine. Serve these with some Fontina Polenta (page 197) or mashed potatoes.

Makes 4 to 6 servings | Active time: 20 minutes | Minimum cook time: 4 hours in a medium slow cooker

4 to 6 (12- to 14-ounce) lamb shanks

3 tablespoons olive oil

1 large sweet onion, diced

1 teaspoon granulated sugar

Salt and freshly ground black pepper to taste

3 garlic cloves, minced

1 tablespoon smoked Spanish paprika

½ cup dried porcini mushrooms

2 cups Beef Stock (page 23)
or purchased stock

2 juice oranges, washed

1½ cups dry red wine

3 tablespoons tomato paste

3 tablespoons chopped fresh rosemary
or 1 tablespoon dried

2 tablespoons chopped fresh parsley

2 bay leaves

1½ tablespoons cornstarch

1. Preheat the oven broiler, and line a broiler pan with heavy-duty aluminum foil. Broil lamb shanks for 3 minutes per side, or until browned. Transfer lamb to the slow cooker, and pour in any juices that have collected in the pan.

2. Heat oil in a skillet over medium heat. Add onion, sugar, salt, and pepper, and toss to coat onions. Cover the pan, and cook for 10 minutes, stirring occasionally. Uncover the pan, and cook over medium-high heat, stirring frequently, for 10 to 15 minutes, or until the onions are browned. Reduce the heat to low, stir in garlic and paprika, and cook for 1 minute, stirring constantly. Scrape mixture into the slow cooker.

3. While onions cook, combine mushrooms and stock in a small saucepan. Bring to a boil over high heat, remove the pan from the heat, and allow mushrooms to soak for 10 minutes. Remove mushrooms from the stock with a slotted spoon, and chop. Strain stock through a sieve lined with a paper coffee filter or paper towel. Add mushrooms and stock to the slow cooker, and stir well.

4. Grate zest from oranges, and squeeze juice from oranges. Add zest and orange juice, wine, tomato paste, rosemary, parsley, and bay leaves to the slow cooker, and stir well. Cook shanks on Low for 8 to 10 hours or on High for 4 to 5 hours, or until lamb is very tender.

5. If cooking on Low, raise the heat to High. Mix cornstarch with 2 tablespoons cold water in a small cup, and add cornstarch mixture to the slow cooker. Cook for an additional 15 to 20 minutes, or until the juices are bubbling and slightly thickened. Remove and discard bay leaves, season to taste with salt and pepper, and serve hot.

Note: The dish can be prepared up to 2 days in advance and refrigerated, tightly covered. Reheat it, covered, in a 350°F oven for 20 to 25 minutes, or until hot.

Variation:
* Substitute short ribs of beef on the bone for the lamb shanks.

Veal Marengo

This dish was invented to celebrate a victory. When Napoleon's troops won the Battle of Marengo on June 14, 1800, his cook, Dunand, produced this in the camp kitchen. The nuance from the orange adds a fresh note to the delicate veal and mushroom stew. Serve it with some brown rice or Wild Rice Pilaf (page 201).

Makes 4 to 6 servings | Active time: 20 minutes | Minimum cook time: 3 hours in a medium slow cooker

1½ pounds veal stew meat

2 tablespoons olive oil

1 large onion, diced

3 garlic cloves, minced

½ pound white mushrooms, rinsed, stemmed, and sliced

1 juice orange, washed

1 (14.5-ounce) can diced tomatoes, undrained

½ cup dry white wine

½ cup Chicken Stock (page 21) or purchased stock

1 tablespoon fresh thyme or ½ teaspoon dried

1 bay leaf

1 tablespoon cornstarch

Salt and freshly ground black pepper to taste

1. Preheat the oven broiler, and line a broiler pan with heavy-duty aluminum foil. Broil beef for 3 minutes per side, or until browned. Transfer veal to the slow cooker, and pour in any juices that have collected in the pan.

2. Heat oil in a medium skillet over medium heat. Add onion, garlic, and mushrooms. Cook, stirring frequently, for 4 to 5 minutes, or until onion is translucent and mushrooms are soft. Scrape mixture into the slow cooker.

3. Grate zest from orange, and squeeze juice from orange. Add zest and orange juice, tomatoes, wine, stock, thyme, and bay leaf to the slow cooker, and stir well. Cook on Low for 6 to 8 hours or on High for 3 to 4 hours, or until veal is tender.

4. If cooking on Low, raise the heat to High. Mix cornstarch and 2 tablespoons cold water in a small cup, and add cornstarch mixture to the slow cooker. Cook for an additional 15 to 20 minutes, or until juices are bubbling and slightly thickened. Remove and discard bay leaf, season to taste with salt and pepper, and serve hot.

Note: The dish can be prepared up to 2 days in advance and refrigerated, tightly covered. Reheat it, covered, over low heat until hot, stirring occasionally.

Variation:

✻ Substitute boneless, skinless chicken thighs for the veal. The cooking time will be the same, and the chicken should be cooked through and no longer pink, and an instant-read thermometer registers 165°F.

Even though citrus fruits might look pristine, there's a chance that there is bacteria or insecticide on them. Wash the fruits with mild soap and water before using them. You won't taste the soap, and it doesn't remove any of the essential oils from the skin of the fruit.

Moroccan Lamb Stew

Contrasting sweet and sour flavors is part of almost all of the world's cuisines. In this stew from North Africa contrasting vinegar and sugar as well as succulent dried apricots and salty olives accomplish this. Serve it over brown rice or Kasha (page 205).

Makes 4 to 6 servings | *Active time: 20 minutes* | *Minimum cooking time: 4 hours in a medium slow cooker*

1½ pounds boneless lamb shoulder, cut into 1½-inch cubes

2 tablespoons olive oil

1 large sweet onion, diced

3 garlic cloves, minced

½ small jalapeño or serrano chile, seeds and ribs removed, and finely chopped

¾ cup dry red wine

¾ cup Beef Stock (page 23) or purchased stock

3 tablespoons balsamic vinegar

2 carrots, cut into thick slices

2 parsnips, cut into thick slices

¼ pound dried apricots, sliced

½ cup sliced pimiento-stuffed green olives

¼ cup firmly packed dark brown sugar

2 tablespoons chopped fresh oregano or 1 tablespoon dried

2 teaspoons ground cumin

1½ tablespoons cornstarch

Salt and freshly ground black pepper to taste

1. Preheat the oven broiler, and line a broiler pan with heavy-duty aluminum foil. Broil lamb for 3 minutes per side, or until browned. Transfer lamb to the slow cooker, and pour in any juices that have collected in the pan.

2. Heat oil in a medium skillet over medium-high heat. Add onion, garlic, and chile. Cook, stirring frequently, for 3 minutes, or until onion is translucent. Scrape mixture into the slow cooker.

3. Add wine, stock, vinegar, carrots, parsnips, dried apricots, olives, brown sugar, oregano, and cumin to the slow cooker, and stir well. Cook shanks on Low for 8 to 10 hours or on High for 4 to 5 hours, or until lamb is very tender.

4. If cooking on Low, raise the heat to High. Mix cornstarch with 2 tablespoons cold water in a small cup, and add cornstarch mixture to the slow cooker. Cook for an additional 15 to 20 minutes, or until the juices are bubbling and slightly thickened. Season to taste with salt and pepper, and serve hot.

Note: The dish can be prepared up to 2 days in advance and refrigerated, tightly covered. Reheat it, covered, over low heat until hot, stirring occasionally.

Variation:

✳ Substitute cubes of beef for the lamb.

> Balsamic vinegar is traditionally made from white Trebbiano grapes grown in the Modena region of Italy. It gets its rich, dark color and mellow flavor from being aged for many years in wooden barrels, similar to aging a wine.

Moussaka

This is one of most famous dishes from Greek cuisine, topping a cinnamon-scented ground lamb and eggplants in a tomato sauce with a custard layer. To make it without gluten, I devised a method for making the white sauce for the custard topping with rice flour and cornstarch. Serve it with a Greek salad.

Makes 4 to 6 servings | Active time: 20 minutes | Minimum cook time: 4 hours in a medium slow cooker

1 (1-pound) eggplant, rinsed, trimmed, and cut into 1-inch cubes

Salt

⅓ cup olive oil

1 large onion, diced

2 garlic cloves, minced

1½ pounds lean ground lamb

⅓ cup dry red wine

1 (8-ounce) can tomato sauce

2 tablespoons chopped fresh parsley

1 tablespoon chopped fresh rosemary or 1 teaspoon dried

1 tablespoon chopped fresh oregano or 1 teaspoon dried

¼ teaspoon ground cinnamon

2 tablespoons unsalted butter

2 tablespoons white rice flour

1 tablespoon cornstarch

1 cup whole milk

2 large eggs, lightly beaten

½ cup crumbled feta cheese

2 tablespoons chopped fresh dill or 2 teaspoons dried

Freshly ground black pepper to taste

1. Place eggplant in a colander, and sprinkle it liberally with salt. Place a plate on top of eggplant, and weight it with cans. Let eggplant sit for 30 minutes, then rinse well, and wring cubes in a cloth towel.

2. Heat half of oil in a large skillet over medium heat. Add eggplant cubes, and cook, stirring frequently, for 5 minutes or until eggplant begins to soften. Transfer eggplant to the slow cooker.

3. Heat remaining oil in the skillet, and add onion and garlic. Cook, stirring frequently, for 3 minutes, or until onion is translucent. Scrape mixture into the slow cooker.

4. Place lamb in the skillet. Brown lamb for 3 to 5 minutes, breaking up any lumps with a fork. Transfer lamb to the slow cooker with a slotted spoon. Add wine, tomato sauce, parsley, rosemary, oregano, and cinnamon to the slow cooker, and stir well. Cook on Low for 5 to 7 hours or on High for 2½ to 3 hours, or until eggplant is tender. Season to taste with salt and pepper.

5. While mixture cooks, prepare topping. Melt butter in a small saucepan over medium heat. Add rice flour and cornstarch, reduce the heat to low, and cook for 2 minutes, stirring constantly. Slowly whisk in the milk, and bring to a boil over medium heat. Reduce the heat to low, and simmer for 2 minutes, or until thickened. Remove the pan from the heat, and allow to cool for 3 minutes. Beat in eggs, cheese, and dill, and season to taste with salt and pepper.

6. When the meat is cooked, if cooking on Low, raise the heat to High. Level meat filling, and pour topping evenly over the top. Cook for 1 to 1½ hours, or until custard is set.

Note: The dish can be prepared up to 2 days in advance and refrigerated, tightly covered. Reheat it, covered, in a 350°F oven for 20 to 25 minutes, or until hot.

Variation:
* Substitute ground beef for the ground lamb.

Veal Paprikash

When anything is labeled "paprikash" it means it's from Hungary and includes tomatoes and sour cream. Serve it with a steamed green vegetable and some rice.

Makes 4 to 6 servings | Active time: 20 minutes | Minimum cook time: 3 hours in a medium slow cooker

1½ pounds veal stew meat

2 tablespoons vegetable oil

2 tablespoons unsalted butter

1 large onion, diced

3 garlic cloves, minced

4 tablespoons paprika, preferably Hungarian

1 (14.5-ounce) can diced tomatoes, undrained

½ cup Chicken Stock (page 21) or purchased stock

½ cup dry white wine

1 tablespoon fresh thyme or ½ teaspoon dried

1½ tablespoons cornstarch

½ cup sour cream

Salt and freshly ground black pepper to taste

1. Preheat the oven broiler, and line a broiler pan with heavy-duty aluminum foil. Broil veal for 3 minutes per side, or until browned. Transfer veal to the slow cooker, and pour in any juices that have collected in the pan.

2. Heat vegetable oil and butter in a large skillet over medium-high heat. Add onion and garlic, and cook, stirring frequently, for 3 minutes, or until onion is translucent. Reduce the heat to low, and stir in paprika. Cook for 1 minute, stirring constantly. Scrape mixture into the slow cooker.

3. Add tomatoes, stock, wine, and thyme to the slow cooker, and stir well. Cook on Low for 6 to 8 hours or on High for 3 to 4 hours, or until veal is tender.

4. If cooking on Low, raise the heat to High. Mix cornstarch and 2 tablespoons cold water in a small cup, and add cornstarch mixture to the slow cooker. Cook for an additional 15 to 20 minutes, or until juices are bubbling and slightly thickened. Stir in sour cream, and cook for 2 to 3 minutes or until sour cream is heated. *Do not let the mixture come to a boil.* Season to taste with salt and pepper, and serve hot.

Note: The dish can be prepared up to 2 days in advance and refrigerated, tightly covered. Reheat it, covered, over low heat until hot, stirring occasionally.

Variation:

✳ Substitute boneless, skinless chicken thighs for the veal. Cook until the chicken is cooked through and registers 165°F on an instant-read thermometer.

> Because sour cream can curdle if it's allowed to boil, always add it at the end of cooking a dish. Stir in the sour cream, and allow the mixture to cook on Low until the juices are once again hot. Then turn off the heat.

Pork Provençal

This vibrant stew punctuated with olives contains many of the flavors common to dishes from this sunny part of southern France, including red bell peppers and leeks. I like to serve it with Fontina Polenta (page 197).

Makes 4 to 6 servings | Active time: 20 minutes | Minimum cook time: 3 1/2 hours in a medium slow cooker

1½ pounds boneless pork loin, cut into 1-inch cubes

4 leeks, white parts only

2 juice oranges, washed

2 tablespoons olive oil

4 garlic cloves, minced

2 red bell peppers, seeds and ribs removed, and thinly sliced

1 (14.5-ounce) can diced tomatoes, drained

1 cup dry white wine

1 cup Chicken Stock (page 21) or purchased stock

¾ cup pitted oil-cured black olives

3 tablespoons chopped fresh parsley

1 tablespoon herbes de Provence

1 bay leaf

1 tablespoon cornstarch

Salt and freshly ground black pepper to taste

1. Preheat the oven broiler, and line a broiler pan with heavy-duty aluminum foil. Broil pork for 3 minutes per side, or until browned. Transfer pork to the slow cooker, and pour in any juices that have collected in the pan.

2. Trim leeks, split lengthwise, and slice thinly. Place slices in a colander and rinse well under cold running water, rubbing with your fingers to dislodge all dirt. Shake leeks in the colander. Grate zest from oranges and squeeze juice from oranges. Set aside.

3. Heat oil in a skillet over medium-high heat. Add leeks, garlic, and red peppers. Cook, stirring frequently, for 3 minutes, or until leeks are translucent. Scrape mixture into the slow cooker.

4. Add tomatoes, orange juice and zest, wine, stock, olives, parsley, herbes de Provence, and bay leaf to the slow cooker, and stir well. Cook on Low for 6 to 8 hours or on High for 3 to 4 hours, or until pork is tender. Remove and discard bay leaf.

5. If cooking on Low, raise the heat to High. Mix cornstarch and 2 tablespoons cold water in a small cup, and add cornstarch mixture to the slow cooker. Cook for an additional 15 to 20 minutes, or until juices are bubbling and slightly thickened. Season to taste with salt and pepper, and serve hot.

Note: The dish can be prepared up to 2 days in advance and refrigerated, tightly covered. Reheat it, covered, over low heat until hot, stirring occasionally.

Variation:

* Substitute 1 (3- to 3½-pound) chicken, cut into serving pieces with the breast halves cut into 2 pieces, for the pork. Cook chicken on Low for 6 to 8 hours or on High for 3 to 4 hours or until chicken is cooked through, tender, and no longer pink.

Pitted olives may be more intention than reality. That's why it's always worth the time to look over pitted olives carefully and not just dump them into a pot. More than one dentist has been called late at night because a patient bit down on an olive to discover a molar-cracking pit.

Greek Beef Stew

Pearl onions and dried currants punctuate the cinnamon-scented red wine sauce of this succulent stew. Serve it with some Kasha (page 205) or Wild Rice Pilaf (page 201) and a tossed salad.

Makes 4 to 6 servings | Active time: 20 minutes | Minimum cook time: 4 hours in a medium slow cooker

2 pounds stewing beef, fat trimmed, and cut into 1-inch cubes

2 tablespoons olive oil

2 medium onions, diced

3 garlic cloves, minced

2 tablespoons chopped fresh oregano or 2 teaspoons dried

½ teaspoon ground cinnamon

½ teaspoon ground coriander

1 juice orange, washed

1 (14.5-ounce) can diced tomatoes, undrained

1 cup Beef Stock (page 23) or purchased stock

½ cup dry red wine

2 tablespoons balsamic vinegar

3 tablespoons firmly packed dark brown sugar

1 (1-pound bag) frozen pearl onions, thawed

¼ cup dried currants

1½ tablespoons cornstarch

Salt and freshly ground black pepper to taste

1. Preheat the oven broiler, and line a broiler pan with heavy-duty aluminum foil. Broil beef for 3 minutes per side, or until browned. Transfer beef to the slow cooker, and pour in any juices that have collected in the pan.

2. Heat oil in a medium skillet over medium-high heat. Add onions and garlic, and cook, stirring frequently, for 3 minutes, or until onions are translucent. Reduce the heat to low, and stir in oregano, cinnamon, and coriander. Cook for 1 minute, stirring constantly. Scrape mixture into the slow cooker.

3. Grate zest from orange, and squeeze juice from orange. Add zest and orange juice, tomatoes, stock, wine, vinegar, brown sugar, pearl onions, and currants to the slow cooker, and stir well. Cook stew on Low for 8 to 10 hours or on High for 4 to 5 hours, or until beef is very tender.

4. If cooking on Low, raise the heat to High. Mix cornstarch with 2 tablespoons cold water in a small cup, and add cornstarch mixture to the slow cooker. Cook for an additional 15 to 20 minutes, or until the juices

are bubbling and slightly thickened. Season to taste with salt and pepper.

Note: The dish can be prepared up to 2 days in advance and refrigerated, tightly covered. Reheat it, covered, in a 350°F oven for 20 to 25 minutes, or until hot.

Variations:

✳ Substitute cubes of boneless lamb shoulder for the beef.

✳ Substitute chopped dried apricots for the dried currants.

> The best way to rid meat dishes of unwanted saturated fat is to chill the dish, then remove and discard the solid layer of fat that will have formed on the top. But if you want to eat the dish the same day it's made, let the dish stand for 10 to 15 minutes, then use a shallow ladle to gather and discard the grease.

Chinese Red-Cooked Pork

Red cooking is a Chinese form of braising that is used primarily in the northern provinces. The pork is simmered with stock and aromatic ingredients and it becomes meltingly tender. Serve it with some stir-fried vegetables and aromatic jasmine rice.

Makes 6 to 8 servings | Active time: 20 minutes | Minimum cook time: 4 hours in a medium slow cooker

1 (2½ to 3-pound) boneless pork shoulder or boneless country ribs

2 tablespoons Asian sesame oil

4 scallions, white parts and 4 inches of green tops, trimmed and sliced

6 garlic cloves, minced

2 tablespoons grated fresh ginger

¾ cup tamari

¾ cup Chicken Stock (page 21) or purchased stock

¼ cup dry sherry

¼ cup firmly packed dark brown sugar

1 teaspoon Chinese five-spice powder

Freshly ground black pepper to taste

1. Preheat the oven broiler, and line a broiler pan with heavy-duty aluminum foil. Broil pork for 3 minutes per side, or until browned. Transfer pork to the slow cooker, and pour in any juices that have collected in the pan.

2. Heat oil in a small skillet over medium-high heat. Add scallions, garlic, and ginger. Cook, stirring frequently, for 2 minutes, or until fragrant. Scrape mixture into a mixing bowl. Add tamari, stock, sherry, brown sugar, and Chinese five-spice powder. Stir well to dissolve sugar, and pour mixture over pork.

3. Cook on Low for 8 to 10 hours or on High for 4 to 5 hours, or until meat is tender. Remove pork from the slow cooker, and keep warm.

4. Pour braising liquid into a saucepan, and cook over high heat until reduced by half. To serve, slice pork against the grain into thin slices, and pass sauce separately.

Note: The dish can be prepared up to 2 days in advance and refrigerated, tightly covered. Reheat it, covered, in a 350°F oven for 20 to 25 minutes, or until hot.

Similar to soy sauce, tamari is a dark sauce made from soy beans. But it has a light and mellow flavor rather than being overwhelmingly salty like soy sauce. The closest substitute is low-sodium Japanese-style soy sauce.

Italian Braised Ham with Vegetables

This is a wonderful way to use up leftover ham. The vegetables and herbs make it more tender as well as taking it away from the realm of a holiday meal. Serve it with Risotto (page 199) or Fontina Polenta (page 197) and a tossed salad.

Makes 4 to 6 servings | Active time: 15 minutes | Minimum cooking time: 3 hours in a medium slow cooker

2 tablespoons olive oil

2 large onions, thinly sliced

3 garlic cloves, minced

1 green bell pepper, seeds and ribs removed, and thinly sliced

1½ pounds baked ham, cut into thick slices

1 (14.5-ounce) can crushed tomatoes in tomato puree

½ cup dry red wine

2 tablespoons chopped fresh parsley

1 tablespoon chopped fresh oregano or 1 teaspoon dried

1 tablespoon chopped fresh basil or 1 teaspoon dried

1 bay leaf

Salt and freshly ground black pepper to taste

1. Heat oil in a medium skillet over medium-high heat. Add onions, garlic, and green bell pepper, and cook, stirring frequently, for 3 minutes, or until onions are translucent. Scrape mixture into the slow cooker.

2. Arrange ham slices over vegetables, and add tomatoes, wine, parsley, oregano, basil, and bay leaf to the slow cooker. Stir well.

3. Cook on Low for 6 to 8 hours or on High for 3 to 4 hours, or until vegetables are tender. Remove and discard bay leaf, season to taste with salt and pepper, and serve hot.

Note: The dish can be prepared up to 2 days in advance and refrigerated, tightly covered. Reheat it, covered, in a 350°F oven for 20 to 25 minutes, or until hot.

> Markets today are drowning in olive oils. They range in price from a few dollars to the equivalent of the gross national product of a Third World nation. The expensive stuff is a condiment and should be drizzled on salads. The cheap stuff is for cooking foods. Not only is it a waste of money to use expensive oil in cooking, it also doesn't work as well.

Choucroute Garnie

This is the best known dish from the Alsace region of France, which borders on Germany and thus sauerkraut is the base of it. Even if you shy away from sauerkraut in general you'll love this dish; the sauerkraut is soaked and then braised to render it sweet and silky. Serve it with steamed potatoes and a green vegetable.

Makes 6 to 8 servings | Prep time: 25 minutes | Minimum cook time: 4 hours in a large slow cooker

3 pounds sauerkraut

2 tablespoons unsalted butter

1 large onion, thinly sliced

1 carrot, thinly sliced

1 cup dry white wine

¼ cup gin (or 10 whole juniper berries)

1 cup Chicken Stock (page 21)
or purchased stock

1 bay leaf

1 pound smoked pork butt,
cut into 1-inch cubes

½ pound kielbasa or other smoked sausage,
cut into 1-inch slices

½ pound bratwurst, knockwurst, or other
unsmoked sausage, cut into 1-inch slices

Salt and freshly ground black pepper
to taste

For serving: variety of mustards

1. Drain sauerkraut in a colander. Place sauerkraut into a large mixing bowl of cold water for 10 minutes. Drain and repeat the soaking. Press out as much water as possible from sauerkraut, and place sauerkraut in the slow cooker.

2. Heat butter in a large skillet over medium-high heat. Add onion and carrot, and cook, stirring frequently, for 3 minutes, or until onion is translucent. Scrape mixture into the slow cooker.

3. Add wine, gin (or berries), stock, and bay leaf to the slow cooker, and stir well. Add pork, kielbasa, and sausage. Press meats down into sauerkraut. Cook on Low for 8 to 10 hours or on High for 4 to 5 hours, or until meats are very tender. Remove and discard bay leaf, and season to taste with salt and pepper. Serve hot, passing a tray of mustards.

Note: The dish can be prepared up to 2 days in advance and refrigerated, tightly covered. Reheat it, covered, in a 350°F oven for 20 to 25 minutes, or until hot.

One step you really don't want to bypass in this recipe is soaking the sauerkraut. Once it's been soaked, the pickled cabbage retains some lip-pursing flavor, but it's quite mild. If you don't soak it, your dish will taste like a pickle that's been heated.

Cajun Stewed Red Beans and Ham

Red beans and rice are a classic in Louisiana, and the ham makes this version even heartier. Serve it with rice and some crunchy coleslaw.

Makes 6 to 8 servings | Active time: 15 minutes | Minimum cook time: 4 hours in a medium slow cooker

1 pound dried red kidney beans

1 (1½-pound) boneless ham steak

2 tablespoons vegetable oil

2 medium onions, finely chopped

2 celery ribs, finely chopped

1 red bell pepper, seeds and ribs removed, and finely chopped

2 garlic cloves, minced

2 bay leaves

2 teaspoon dried thyme

4 cups water

Salt and cayenne to taste

1 cup corn kernels, cooked

1. Rinse beans in a colander and place them in a mixing bowl covered with cold water. Allow beans to soak for at least six hours, or overnight. Or place beans into a saucepan and bring to a boil over high heat. Boil 1 minute. Turn off the heat, cover the pan, and soak beans for 1 hour. With either soaking method, drain beans, discard soaking water, and begin cooking as soon as possible.

2. Trim ham of all visible fat, and cut ham into 1-inch cubes. Heat oil in a skillet over medium-high heat. Add ham cubes, and brown on all sides. Transfer ham to the slow cooker with a slotted spoon. Add onions, celery, bell pepper, and garlic to the skillet. Cook, stirring frequently, for 3 minutes, or until onions are translucent. Scrape mixture into the slow cooker.

3. Add bay leaves, thyme, and water to the slow cooker, and stir well. Cook on Low for 8 to 10 hours or on High for 4 to 5 hours, or until beans are very tender. Remove and discard bay leaves, season to taste with salt and cayenne, and serve hot, garnished with corn kernels.

Note: The dish can be prepared up to 2 days in advance and refrigerated, tightly covered. Reheat it, covered, over low heat until hot, stirring occasionally.

Variations:

∗ Substitute andouille sausage or smoked kielbasa for the ham.

∗ Add 1 or 2 jalapeño or serrano chiles, seeds and ribs removed, and finely chopped, to the recipe. Saute them along with the other vegetables.

> Jazz great Louis Armstrong, whose name is synonymous with New Orleans jazz, used to sign his letters "Red beans and ricely yours."

Mexican Frittata

There are two types of chorizo: a raw bulk sausage and a hard, ready-to-eat sausage. This brightly flavored frittata uses raw chorizo, and its spicy flavor permeates the dish to deliver eggs with a punch. Some Cowboy Beans (page 203) or Refried Beans (page 209) and rice go with it well.

Makes 4 to 6 servings | Active time: 20 minutes | Minimum cook time: 2 hours in a medium slow cooker

½ pound bulk chorizo sausage

1 medium onion, chopped

2 garlic cloves, minced

½ green bell pepper, seeds and ribs removed, and chopped

1 tablespoon ground cumin

1 teaspoon dried oregano

8 large eggs

¼ cup half-and-half

½ cup grated jalapeño Jack cheese

1 (4-ounce) can chopped mild green chiles, drained

¾ cup canned red kidney beans, drained and rinsed

Salt and freshly ground black pepper to taste

Vegetable oil spray

1. Place chorizo in a skillet over medium-high heat. Cook for 5 to 7 minutes, breaking up lumps with a fork, or until sausage is browned. Remove sausage from the pan with a slotted spoon, drain on paper towels, and set aside.

2. Discard all but 2 tablespoons fat from the skillet. Add onion, garlic, and green bell pepper, and cook for 5 minutes, or until vegetables soften. Add cumin and oregano, and cook for 1 minute, stirring constantly. Allow mixture to cool for 5 minutes.

3. Whisk eggs with half-and-half in a mixing bowl. Stir in cooled vegetables, cheese, chiles, and beans, and season to taste with salt and pepper.

4. Grease the inside of the slow cooker insert liberally with vegetable oil spray or melted butter. Fold a sheet of heavy-duty aluminum foil in half, and place it in the bottom of the slow cooker with the sides of the foil extending up the sides of the slow cooker. Pour egg mixture into the slow cooker.

5. Cook on High for 2 to 2½ hours, or until eggs are set. Run a spatula around the sides of the slow cooker. Remove frittata from the slow cooker by pulling it up by the sides of the foil. Slide it gently onto a serving platter, and cut it into wedges. Serve immediately, or at room temperature.

Note: The vegetable mixture can be cooked up to 1 day in advance and refrigerated, tightly covered. Reheat the vegetables to room temperature in a microwave-safe dish, or over low heat, before completing the dish.

Variation:

✳ For a milder dish, substitute Monterey Jack for the jalapeño Jack, and omit the chiles.

Grating cheese is a snap in a food processor fitted with a steel blade. If you're doing it by hand with a box grater, spray the grater with vegetable oil spray, and the cheese will grate far more easily.

Cassoulet

There are certain "comfort foods" that I cook at least once every winter, and this hearty dish made with lamb, sausage, duck, and stewed beans is one of them. A salad is all you need on the plate with this one-dish dinner.

Makes 6 to 8 servings | Prep time: 30 minutes | Minimum cook time: 5 1/2 hours in a large slow cooker

1 pound flageolet or other small dried beans such as navy beans

2 tablespoons olive oil

2 large onions, diced

5 garlic cloves, minced

2 cups Chicken Stock (page 21) or purchased stock

1 cup dry white wine

1 (14.5-ounce) can diced tomatoes, undrained

3 tablespoons tomato paste

1 tablespoon herbes de Provence (or 1 teaspoon dried thyme, 1 teaspoon dried rosemary, and 1 teaspoon dried oregano)

1 bay leaf

1 pound stewing lamb, cut into 1-inch cubes

1 pound kielbasa or other smoked pork sausage, cut into ½-inch slices

½ pound roasted duck, boned and diced

Salt and freshly ground black pepper to taste

1. Rinse beans in a colander and place them in a mixing bowl covered with cold water. Allow beans to soak for at least six hours, or overnight. Or place beans into a saucepan and bring to a boil over high heat. Boil 1 minute. Turn off the heat, cover the pan, and soak beans for 1 hour. With either soaking method, drain beans, discard soaking water, and begin cooking as soon as possible.

2. Heat oil in a medium skillet over medium-high heat. Add onions and garlic, and cook, stirring frequently, for 3 minutes, or until onions are translucent. Scrape mixture into the slow cooker.

3. Add stock, wine, tomatoes, tomato paste, herbes de Provence, and bay leaf to the slow cooker, and stir well. Cook bean mixture for 4 hours on Low or 2 hours on High.

4. Preheat the oven broiler, and line a broiler pan with heavy-duty aluminum foil. Broil lamb and kielbasa for 3 minutes per side, or until browned. Stir meats into the slow cooker along with any juices that have accumulated in the pan. Cook for 5 to 7 hours on Low or 3 to 4 hours on High, or until lamb is tender.

5. Stir roasted duck meat into the slow cooker. Cook for an additional 15 to 20 minutes, or until duck is hot. Remove and discard bay leaf, season to taste with salt and pepper, and serve hot.

Note: The dish can be prepared up to 2 days in advance and refrigerated, tightly covered. Reheat it, covered, in a 350°F oven for 20 to 25 minutes, or until hot.

Cassoulet goes back centuries and is one of the culinary triumphs of southwest France, with most authorities citing Castelnaudary in the Languedoc province as its birthplace. Beans and a variety of meats are always part of the dish, but there are many versions. Duck or goose confit (in which the meat is cured in its own fat) is a traditional ingredient, because confit is popular in southwestern France. Other traditional ingredients, such mutton, partridge, various cuts of pork, and sausages, are a matter of regional debate.

Feijoada

You could think of this dish as tropical version of Cassoulet (page 187). A combination of hearty black beans with sausages, all scented with orange, it holds the distinction of being the national dish of Brazil. Serve it over rice with a tossed salad on the side.

Makes 6 to 8 servings | Active time: 25 minutes | Minimum cook time: 4 hours in a medium slow cooker

1 pound dried black beans

2 tablespoons olive oil

½ pound kielbasa, cut into 1-inch pieces

½ pound chorizo, cut into 1-inch pieces

½ pound bratwurst, cut into 1-inch slices

½ pound ham steak, trimmed of fat and cut into 1-inch pieces

3 large onions, diced

5 garlic cloves, minced

1 red bell pepper, seeds and ribs removed, and chopped

5 cups water

1 navel orange, cut into quarters

3 bay leaves

Salt and freshly ground black pepper to taste

FOR GARNISH:

1 navel orange, sliced

1 cup homemade or refrigerated tomato salsa

1 cup shredded green cabbage, blanched for 5 minutes

1. Rinse beans in a colander and place them in a mixing bowl covered with cold water. Allow beans to soak for at least six hours, or overnight. Or place beans into a saucepan and bring to a boil over high heat. Boil 1 minute. Turn off the heat, cover the pan, and soak beans for 1 hour. With either soaking method, drain beans, discard soaking water, and begin cooking as soon as possible.

2. Heat oil in a large skillet over medium-high heat. Add kielbasa, chorizo, bratwurst, and ham, and cook, stirring frequently, until sausages are browned. Remove meat from the pan with a slotted spoon, and transfer them to the slow cooker. Add onions, garlic, and red bell pepper to the skillet. Cook, stirring frequently, for 3 minutes, or until onion is translucent. Scrape mixture into the slow cooker.

3. Add beans, water, orange, and bay leaves to the slow cooker, and stir well. Cook on Low for 8 to 10 hours or on High for 4 to 5 hours, or until beans are very tender. Remove and discard orange quarters and bay leaves.

4. Transfer 1 cup of beans and ½ cup of cooking liquid to food processor fitted with the steel blade or to a blender. Puree until smooth, and stir mixture back into the slow cooker. Season to taste with salt and pepper, and serve hot, passing bowls of garnish foods separately.

Note: The dish can be prepared up to 2 days in advance and refrigerated, tightly covered. Reheat it, covered, in a 350°F oven for 20 to 25 minutes, or over low heat, stirring occasionally, until hot.

Variation:

✳ Substitute kidney beans for the black beans, substitute Andouille sausage and Chorizo for sausages listed, and omit orange in cooking process for a Cajun version of this dish.

The reason why it's important to start cooking beans as soon as the soaking time passes is because bacteria can form in warm or even room temperature water and the beans will begin to ferment. The other caveat of bean cookery is to make sure beans are cooked to the proper consistency before adding any acidic ingredient, such as tomatoes or lemon. The acid prevents the beans from becoming tender.

Chapter 8

Side Dish Stars:

Rice, Grains, Vegetables, and Sauces

The spotlight shining on a dinner plate should focus on one dish. If the centerpiece of the plate is an elaborate dish like a stew or meat with a sauce, then the accompaniments should be planned to harmonize with that option. But when the entrée is a simple piece of baked, broiled, or grilled food, then it's the side dishes that make the meal memorable. Those are the recipes you'll find in this chapter.

At the beginning of the chapter are a few sections on basic ways to use the slow cooker as the indispensable tool it is for basic foods such as rice and beans. These two gluten-free categories of food are the mainstays of diets the world over. Then there are recipes for specific dishes with suggestions for what types of foods they best complement.

Slow-Cooking Rice

There are literally thousands of species of rice, which makes it the world's most popular grain; all species trace their lineage to India. When rice comes from the field, it is termed "paddy rice," and it must have the non-edible hull removed before it can be eaten. Brown rice is whole or broken kernels of rice from which only the hull has been removed. For white rice, the grains are rubbed together to remove this natural bran.

In the same way that small slow cookers can double as fondue pots, any size slow cooker can take the place of an electric rice cooker, which is a fixture in almost all Asian homes. The main difference when cooking rice in the slow cooker is that less water is used. That's because it doesn't evaporate as quickly as when cooking rice conventionally. Brown rice takes longer to cook so you'll use a bit more water to compensate for eventual evaporation. I usually season rice with salt and pepper after it's cooked, but I add butter at the beginning of the cooking process. The butter lubricates the rice grains so they don't become gummy and stick together.

White Rice Cooking Chart

RICE	WATER	BUTTER	SERVES	HIGH
1 cup	1 $^3/_4$ cups	1 tablespoon	4	1 $^1/_2$ hours
2 cups	3 $^1/_3$ cups	2 tablespoons	8	2 hours
3 cups	4 $^1/_4$ cups	3 tablespoons.	12	2 $^1/_4$ hours

Brown Rice Cooking Chart

RICE	WATER	BUTTER	SERVES	HIGH
1 cup	2 cups	1 tablespoons	4	2 $^1/_2$ hours
2 cups	3 $^2/_3$ cups	2 tablespoons	8	3 hours
3 cups	4 $^3/_4$ cups	3 tablespoons	12	3 $^3/_4$ hours

Rice is classified primarily by the size of the grain. Long grains are five times longer than they are wide, and when cooked, the grains tend to remain separate. Medium grains are plump in shape, but not round, and when cooked, medium grain rice tends to be more moist and tender than long grain. Used for sushi and other Japanese dishes, short grain rice appears almost round in shape, and when cooked tends to cling together, which is why it's sometimes called sticky rice.

Other Gluten-Free Grains

Back in the Pleistocene Era of the 1970s when I first used a slow cooker, rice was really synonymous with grains, and it was even difficult to find brown rice apart from incense-scented health food stores. But that is hardly the case today, and many nutritious whole grains are part of a gluten-free

diet. There are specific recipes given for buckwheat groats, better known as Kasha (page 205) and Wild Rice Pilaf (page 201).

The grain that is skyrocketing in popularity today, however, is quinoa. This grain, pronounced *KEEN-wah,* is native to the Peruvian Andes and is valued for its high protein content, and it contains a balanced set of essential amino acids, which makes it a complete source of protein. Quinoa should always be rinsed well before cooking, and it should be cooked according to the timing given above for brown rice.

Basics for Dried Beans

Slow cookers are perfect for cooking beans and pulses; keep in mind that the slow cookers of today represent the evolution of the classic bean pot. The first step for all bean recipes is to rinse the beans in a sieve or colander, and look them over carefully to discard any broken beans or the occasional pebble that sneaks into the bag. Also, keep in mind when you're cooking beans to not fill the slow cooker more than one third with beans because they more than double in volume once they're cooked.

Although guidelines are given for how long each bean recipe takes to cook, there are variables that influence this time. If beans are a few years old, they'll take longer to cook. Also, the minerals in your tap water can retard the softening and require a longer cooking time, as can the addition of sweeteners such as maple syrup or acids such as tomatoes or wine.

With the exception of lentils and split peas, all beans should be soaked before cooking. For many years, it was believed that soaking was beneficial because the enzymes that make beans difficult for some people to digest leach out into the soaking water, which is then discarded. Lately, researchers have questioned whether the amount of enzyme removed in this way is significant. Most cooks agree, however, that soaking does soften the beans and save cooking time.

Cooking beans is common sense; the larger the bean the longer it will take to soften. But it's not necessary to pre-soak larger beans for a longer period of

Keep in mind that beans should always be covered with liquid at all times while they're cooking, so towards the end of the cooking process take a look and add boiling water if the water seems almost evaporated.

time than smaller beans. There's only so much softening that goes on at no or low heat. Beans need to be gently simmered, and that's why the slow cooker is your best friend. It's far more patient than any pot on a stove to accomplish this task.

Once you've soaked the beans, place them in the slow cooker and cover them with very hot tap water by at least three inches. Here's a chart to tell you how long it will take to make them tender. The chart is based on two cups of dried beans, which yields six cups of cooked beans:

Bean Cooking Chart

BEAN TYPE	TIME ON HIGH
Black beans	3 hours
Black-eyed peas	$3 \frac{1}{4}$ hours
Fava beans	2 3/4 hours
Garbanzo beans	$3 \frac{1}{2}$ hours
Great Northern beans	$2 \frac{3}{4}$ hours
Kidney beans	3 hours
Lentils	2 hours (no presoaking)
Lima beans	$2 \frac{1}{2}$ for baby, $3 \frac{1}{2}$ for large
Navy beans	$2 \frac{1}{2}$ hours
Split peas	$2 \frac{1}{2}$ hours (no presoaking)
White beans	3 hours

Substituting Beans

Some dried beans are more difficult to find than others; for example, I frequently need a substitution for French flageolet. But sometimes I want to make a substitution for aesthetic reasons. If serving a pale chicken dish I might want to change a navy bean recipe to use dark red kidney beans to add a contrasting color to the plate.

Of the legumes, garbanzo beans are one that really has no appropriate stand-in. This specie of bean is far "meatier" in texture, and has a nutlike flavor that cannot be replicated. That's why it's not included in the following substitution chart.

NAME OF LEGUME	WHAT TO SUBSTITUTE
Black (also called Turtle)	Kidney
Black-eyed peas	Kidney
Cannellini	Navy
Cranberry	Kidney
Fava (broad beans)	Large lima
Flageolet	Navy
Kidney (pink and red, pinto)	Navy
Lentils (red, brown, green)	Split peas
Split peas	Lentils

Although many dried beans can be substituted for one another, don't substitute with canned beans in the slow cooker. Canned beans are already fully cooked, and they'll fall apart before they absorb the flavoring from the slow-cooked dish.

Fontina Polenta

Polenta is a relative newcomer to the world of Italian cuisine because all corn was imported from the New World. But it's now a gluten-free staple and can be adapted to many cuisines and times of day. Serve polenta instead of an English muffin as the base for eggs Benedict, or make it American and serve it at breakfast in place of grits.

Makes 4 to 6 servings | Prep time: 10 minutes | Minimum cook time: 3 hours in a medium slow cooker

5 cups Chicken Stock (page 21) or purchased stock

1 cup half-and-half

1 cup polenta or yellow cornmeal

1 tablespoon fresh thyme or ½ teaspoon dried

3 tablespoons unsalted butter, cut into small pieces

1 cup grated Fontina cheese

Salt and freshly ground black pepper to taste

Vegetable oil spray

1. Grease the inside of the slow cooker liberally with vegetable oil spray.

2. Combine stock, half-and-half, polenta, and thyme in the slow cooker. Whisk well, and cook on High for 1½ hours, or until mixture begins to boil.

3. Whisk well again, and cook on High for an additional 1½ hours or on Low for 3 hours, or until polenta is very thick.

4. Stir in butter and cheese, and season to taste with salt and pepper. Serve immediately as a side dish or topped with sauce. The polenta can remain on Warm for up to 4 hours.

Note: The dish can be prepared up to 2 days in advance and refrigerated, tightly covered. Reheat it, covered, in a 350°F oven for 20 to 25 minutes, or until hot.

Variations:

* Substitute jalapeño Jack for the Fontina, and add 1 (4-ounce) can diced mild green chiles to the slow cooker.
* Add 2 tablespoons chopped fresh herbs, such as sage, rosemary, or thyme at the onset of the cooking time.
* Add ½ cup dried porcini mushrooms, broken into small pieces and rinsed, to the slow cooker, and stir in 1 tablespoon truffle oil at the end of the cooking time.
* Add 1 (14.5-ounce) can diced tomatoes, undrained, 1 tablespoon tomato paste, and 2 tablespoons chopped fresh basil or oregano to the slow cooker, and reduce the amount of stock to 3 cups.

* Substitute sharp cheddar for the Fontina, and add ¼ pound bacon, cooked until crisp and crumbled, to the slow cooker when whisking halfway through the cooking time.
* Add 1 cup fresh corn kernels or frozen corn, thawed, to the slow cooker when whisking the polenta halfway through the cooking time.

An alternative way to serve polenta is to pack the hot polenta into a well-oiled loaf pan and chill it well. Once chilled you can cut it into ¾-inch slices and either grill them or saute them in butter or olive oil. You can also spread the polenta in a shallow baking dish to a thickness of ¾ inch, and then chill the mixture, cut it into long narrow rectangles, and pan-fry them.

Risotto

I could write a whole book on just variations of risotto, and once you've made it in the slow cooker you'll never stand at a stove stirring again. The quantity made by this recipe creates a side dish, either served as the pasta course or alongside a simple piece of fish, poultry, or meat. However, if you want to serve it as the entrée itself, this quantity should be increased for the number of servings.

Makes 4 to 6 servings | *Prep time: 15 minutes* | *Minimum cook time: 2 hours in a medium slow cooker*

3 tablespoons unsalted butter

1 medium onion, chopped

1 cup Arborio rice

½ cup dry white wine

2½ cups Chicken Stock (page 21) or purchased stock

½ cup freshly grated Parmesan cheese

Salt and freshly ground black pepper to taste

1. Heat butter in a medium saucepan over medium-high heat. Add onion and cook, stirring frequently, for 3 minutes, or until onion is translucent. Add rice and stir to coat grains. Raise the heat to high and add wine. Stir for 2 minutes, or until wine is almost evaporated. Scrape mixture into the slow cooker.

2. Add stock to the slow cooker, and stir well. Cook on High for 2 hours, or until rice is soft and liquid is absorbed. Stir in cheese, season to taste with salt and pepper, and serve hot.

Note: The dish can be prepared up to 2 days in advance and refrigerated, tightly covered. Reheat it, covered, in a 350°F oven for 20 to 25 minutes, or until hot.

Variations:

* Add 2 tablespoons chopped dried mushrooms, and ½ pound sauteed mushrooms, or a combination of white and wild mushrooms at the onset of the cooking time.
* Add ½ cup crumbled gorgonzola cheese along with the Parmesan.
* Add ½ pound fresh asparagus, cut into 1-inch sections, to the slow cooker 1½ hours into the cooking time.
* Add 1 cup butternut squash, peeled and cut into ½-inch cubes, to the slow cooker at the onset of the cooking time.
* Substitute beef stock for the chicken stock, and substitute red wine for the white wine.
* Add 2 tablespoons tomato paste to the slow cooker, and add 2 tablespoons chopped fresh oregano and 1 tablespoon chopped fresh basil.
* Substitute seafood stock for the chicken stock, and stir 1 cup diced cooked lobster or shrimp into the slow cooker at the end of the cooking time.

Risotto is one of Milan's contributions to Italian cuisine, and legend has it that it originated in the sixteenth century. True risotto *alla milanese* is made with saffron, which perfumes the rice and creates a pale yellow dish. Today, almost any creamy rice dish with cheese added is called a risotto, but the authentic dish is made with Arborio rice, which, when cooked, releases a starch and creates its own sauce. The traditional dish requires constant stirring—a step happily unnecessary with the slow cooker version.

Wild Rice Pilaf

Wild rice is has such a wonderful nutty flavor, and it pairs well with both poultry and meats. You can also use it as a stuffing for poultry, and it makes a wonderful cold salad too.

Makes 4 to 6 servings | *Prep time: 15 minutes* | *Minimum cook time: 3 hours in a medium slow cooker*

3 tablespoons unsalted butter

1 large onion, chopped

1 carrot, chopped

1 cup wild rice, rinsed

¼ cup dried currants

3 cups Vegetable Stock (page 24), Chicken Stock (page 21) or purchased stock

Salt and freshly ground black pepper to taste

1. Melt butter in a small skillet over medium-high heat. Add onion and carrot, and cook, stirring frequently, for 3 minutes, or until onion is translucent. Scrape mixture into the slow cooker.

2. Add wild rice, currants, and stock to the slow cooker, and stir well. Cook on Low for 7 to 8 hours or on High for 3 to 4 hours, or until rice is fluffed and tender and stock is absorbed. Season to taste with salt and pepper, and serve hot.

Note: The dish can be prepared up to 2 days in advance and refrigerated, tightly covered. Reheat it, covered, in a 350ºF oven for 20 to 25 minutes, or until hot.

Variation:

* Substitute raisins or chopped dried apricots for the dried currants.

Wild rice is a grain named *Zizania palustris*, and is not officially a species of rice. It's harvested primarily by Native Americans in states such as Minnesota and certain provinces of Canada. The groups paddle canoes to the plants and then bend down the ripe grain heads with wooden sticks called knockers to extract the seeds. Some tribes, such as the Ojibwa, consider the grain sacred.

Cowboy Beans

In the Southwest beans are served soupy and wet, and that's how these flavorful kidney beans end up. They're great with any meats cooked on the grill, or roasted poultry too.

Makes 6 to 8 servings | Prep time: 15 minutes | Minimum cook time: 3 hours in a medium slow cooker

1 pound dried kidney beans

3 tablespoons olive oil

1 large onion, diced

½ green bell pepper, seeds and ribs removed, and chopped

3 garlic cloves, minced

1 jalapeño or serrano chile, seeds and ribs removed, and finely chopped

2 tablespoons chili powder

2 tablespoons smoked Spanish paprika

1 tablespoon ground cumin

2 teaspoons dried oregano

4 cups Vegetable Stock (page 24) or purchased stock

2 bay leaves

Salt and freshly ground black pepper to taste

1. Rinse beans in a colander and place them in a mixing bowl covered with cold water. Allow beans to soak for at least six hours, or overnight. Or place beans into a saucepan and bring to a boil over high heat. Boil 1 minute. Turn off the heat, cover the pan, and soak beans for 1 hour. With either soaking method, drain beans, discard soaking water, and begin cooking as soon as possible.

2. Heat oil in a skillet over medium-high heat. Add onion, bell pepper, garlic, and chile, and cook, stirring frequently, for 3 minutes, or until onion is translucent. Reduce the heat to low, and stir in chili powder, paprika, cumin, and oregano. Cook for 1 minute, stirring constantly. Scrape mixture into the slow cooker.

3. Add drained beans, stock, and bay leaves to the slow cooker, and stir well. Cook on Low for 6 to 8 hours or on High for 3 to 4 hours, or until beans are tender. Remove and discard bay leaves, season to taste with salt and pepper, and serve hot.

Note: The dish can be prepared up to 2 days in advance and refrigerated, tightly covered. Reheat it, covered, in a 350°F oven for 20 to 25 minutes, or until hot.

Variation:

❋ Substitute pinto beans or black beans for the kidney beans.

As garlic gets older bitter green shoots begin to emerge from the individual cloves. Never buy a head if the shoots are visible, and for a recipe like this one don't use heads if you see green shoots after cutting off the top of the head. You don't have to discard the heads; break them into individual cloves and remove the green centers before chopping or mincing.

Kasha (Buckwheat Groats)

People on gluten-free diets need to remember that buckwheat is not a relative of the wheat that is off limits, and once toasted and braised it has a nutlike flavor and wonderful aroma. Serve it with hearty poultry and meat dishes.

Makes 4 to 6 servings | *Prep time: 15 minutes* | *Minimum cook time: 2 hours in a medium slow cooker*

1 large egg

Pinch of salt

1 cup coarse kasha

2 tablespoons olive oil

1 small onion, chopped

1 garlic clove, minced

2 cups Chicken Stock (page 21) or purchased stock

2 tablespoons chopped fresh parsley

2 teaspoons fresh thyme or ¼ teaspoon dried

Freshly ground black pepper to taste

Vegetable oil spray

1. Grease the inside of the slow cooker liberally with vegetable oil spray.

2. Whisk the egg in a small bowl with the salt. Stir in the kasha, making sure that all grains are coated, and set aside.

3. Heat the oil in a skillet over medium-high heat. Add onion and garlic, and cook, stirring frequently, for 3 minutes, or until onion is translucent. Add kasha, and stir for 3 to 4 minutes, or until grains dry. Scrape mixture into the slow cooker.

4. Add stock, parsley, and thyme to the slow cooker, and stir well. Cook on High for 2 to 2½ hours, or until liquid is absorbed. Season to taste with salt and pepper, and serve hot.

Note: The dish can be prepared up to 2 days in advance and refrigerated, tightly covered. Reheat it, covered, in a 350°F oven for 20 to 25 minutes, or until hot.

Variation:

* Add ½ cup dried porcini mushrooms, broken into small pieces and rinsed, to the slow cooker.

> Braising buckwheat groats is a dish native to Russia, and while by the eighteenth century it was a peasant dish, it began as a dish for the nobility. From the twelfth to fourteenth centuries the word *kasha* was almost synonymous with the word *feast*.

Old-Fashioned New England Baked Beans

Here's a recipe for all seasons, especially since making it in the summer to serve at grill-outs doesn't involve heating up the kitchen by lighting the oven. This version is the way I think the dish should be prepared, sweet and thick.

Makes 6 to 8 servings | Prep time: 15 minutes | Minimum cook time: 4 hours in a medium slow cooker

1 pound dried navy beans

¼ pound bacon, cut into 1-inch lengths

1 small red onion, diced

2½ cups water

½ cup firmly packed dark brown sugar

½ cup cider vinegar

½ cup Gingered Barbecue Sauce (page 221) or gluten-free prepared barbecue sauce

1 tablespoon mustard powder

1 tablespoon tomato paste

¾ cup grated Monterey Jack cheese

Salt and freshly ground black pepper to taste

1. Rinse beans in a colander and place them in a mixing bowl covered with cold water. Allow beans to soak for at least six hours, or overnight. Or place beans into a saucepan and bring to a boil over high heat. Boil 1 minute. Turn off the heat, cover the pan, and soak beans for 1 hour. With either soaking method, drain beans, discard soaking water, and begin cooking as soon as possible.

2. Cook bacon in a heavy skillet over medium-high heat for 5 to 7 minutes, or until crisp. Remove bacon from the pan with a slotted spoon, and transfer it to the slow cooker. Discard all but 2 tablespoons bacon grease. Add onion to the skillet, and cook, stirring frequently, for 3 minutes, or until onion is translucent. Scrape onion into the slow cooker.

3. Add water, brown sugar, vinegar, onion, bacon, barbecue sauce, mustard, and tomato paste to the slow cooker, and stir well. Cook on Low for 8 to 10 hours or on High for 4 to 5 hours, or until beans are tender.

4. If cooking on Low, raise the heat to High. Stir in cheese, and season to taste with salt and pepper. Cook for an additional 10 to 20 minutes, or until cheese melts, and serve hot.

Note: The dish can be prepared up to 2 days in advance and refrigerated, tightly covered. Reheat it, covered, in a 350°F oven for 20 to 25 minutes, or until hot.

During the Colonial era, the Puritans would prepare baked beans on Saturday and serve them for dinner that night and for lunch on Sunday because no cooking was allowed on the Sabbath. The beans were cooked in a pot in the embers of the fire over low heat for a long time—like a slow cooker. Baked beans are so interwoven into the history of Boston that the nickname remains "Beantown."

Refried Beans

Refried beans, called *frijoles refritos* south of the border, is an authentic Mexican dish. In this version they gain a smoky nuance by including both smoked paprika and chipotle chiles. They go with any meal that contains other Hispanic flavors.

Makes 6 to 8 servings | *Prep time: 20 minutes* | *Minimum cook time: 4 1/2 hours in a medium slow cooker*

1 pound dried red kidney beans

1/2 cup vegetable oil or bacon fat

2 large red onions, diced

6 garlic cloves, minced

2 jalapeño or serrano chiles, seeds and ribs removed, and finely chopped

2 tablespoons smoked Spanish paprika

1 tablespoon ground cumin

1 teaspoon dried oregano

1 chipotle chile in adobo sauce, finely chopped

1/2 cup refrigerated commercial tomato salsa

Salt and cayenne to taste

1. Rinse beans in a colander and place them in a mixing bowl covered with cold water. Allow beans to soak for at least six hours, or overnight. Or place beans into a saucepan and bring to a boil over high heat. Boil 1 minute. Turn off the heat, cover the pan, and soak beans for 1 hour. With either soaking method, drain beans, discard soaking water, and begin cooking as soon as possible.

2. Add 6 cups water to the slow cooker, and cook on Low for 8 to 10 hours or on High for 4 to 5 hours, or until beans are very tender and beginning to fall apart. Remove beans from the slow cooker with a slotted spoon, and reserve 1/2 cup cooking liquid.

3. Heat oil in a large skillet over medium-high heat. Add onions, garlic, and fresh chiles, and cook, stirring frequently, for 4 to 5 minutes, or until onions are soft. Reduce the heat to low, and stir in paprika, cumin, and oregano. Cook for 1 minute, stirring constantly.

4. Stir in beans, reserved bean cooking liquid, chipotle chile, and salsa. Mash beans with a potato masher or the back of a heavy spoon until beans are soft but some beans still remain whole. Season to taste with salt and pepper, and serve hot.

Note: The dish can be prepared up to 2 days in advance and refrigerated, tightly covered. Reheat it, covered, in a 350°F oven for 20 to 25 minutes, or until hot.

Variation:

✱ Substitute black beans for the kidney beans.

Some cookbooks tell you to wear rubber gloves when handling hot chiles. That's not really necessary (unless you have sensitive skin), but you do need to take care. I cut the chilies on a glass plate rather than on my cutting board so the volatile oils do not penetrate. What's most important is that you wash your hands thoroughly after handling chiles.

Asian Butternut Squash

This dish has a permanent home on my Thanksgiving table, and the addition of orange zest and aromatic Chinese five-spice powder add complexity to the taste. Apart from turkey and other poultry, it's great with pork too.

Makes 6 to 8 servings | Prep time: 15 minutes | Minimum cook time: 3 hours in a medium slow cooker

1 (2½-pound) butternut squash, peeled and cut into ½-inch cubes

½ cup hoisin sauce

¼ cup freshly squeezed orange juice

1 tablespoon soy sauce

1 tablespoon grated orange zest

3 tablespoons unsalted butter, melted

½ teaspoon Chinese five-spice powder

Salt and freshly ground black pepper to taste

1. Place squash in the slow cooker. Combine hoisin sauce, orange juice, soy sauce, orange zest, melted butter, and Chinese five-spice powder in a small mixing bowl. Stir well, and pour the mixture over squash.

2. Cook on Low for 6 to 8 hours or on High for 3 to 4 hours, or until squash is tender. For chunky squash, mash cubes with a potato masher right in the slow cooker. For smooth squash, spoon the contents of the slow cooker into a food processor fitted with a steel blade, and puree until smooth using on-and-off pulsing. Season to taste with salt and pepper, and serve hot.

Note: The dish can be prepared up to 2 days in advance and refrigerated, tightly covered. Reheat it, covered, in a 350°F oven for 20 to 25 minutes, or until hot.

Variation:

* Substitute molasses for the hoisin sauce and cinnamon for the Chinese five-spice powder.

One of the greatest advances of civilization is already-peeled butternut squash in the produce section of supermarkets, especially during the fall and winter. If you buy it, the prep time for this or any other winter squash recipe is about three minutes.

Braised Red Cabbage

This Austrian recipe is my favorite side dish for hearty meat and game dishes in the winter. The cabbage is slightly sweet from the apple and jam, and the slow cooker makes it meltingly tender.

Makes 8 to 10 servings | *Prep time: 15 minutes* | *Minimum cook time: 3 hours in a medium slow cooker*

1 (2-pound) red cabbage, cored and shredded

2 tablespoons red wine vinegar

2 tablespoons granulated sugar

3 tablespoons unsalted butter, divided

1 medium onion, chopped

1 apple, peeled and chopped

½ cup dry red wine

½ cup Vegetable Stock (page 24) or purchased stock

1 (3-inch) cinnamon stick

1 bay leaf

½ cup red currant jelly

Salt and freshly ground black pepper to taste

1. Rinse cabbage and cut it into quarters. Discard core from each quarter and shred cabbage. Place cabbage in the slow cooker, sprinkle with vinegar and sugar, and toss to coat.

2. Heat 2 tablespoons butter in a medium skillet over medium-high heat. Add onion and apple, and cook, stirring frequently, for 3 minutes, or until onion is translucent. Scrape mixture into the slow cooker.

3. Add wine, stock, cinnamon stick, and bay leaf into the slow cooker, and stir well. Cook on Low for 6 to 8 hours or on High for 3 to 4 hours, or until cabbage is almost tender.

4. If cooking on Low, raise the heat to High. Remove and discard cinnamon stick and bay leaf, and stir jelly and remaining butter into cabbage. Cook on High for an additional 30 to 40 minutes, or until cabbage is tender and glazed. Season to taste with salt and pepper, and serve immediately.

Note: The dish can be prepared up to 2 days in advance and refrigerated, tightly covered. Reheat it, covered, over low heat until hot, stirring occasionally.

> Using cinnamon sticks rather than ground cinnamon in dishes creates a subtler cinnamon flavor. If you only have ground cinnamon, substitute ½ teaspoon for each 3-inch cinnamon stick specified.

Southern Stewed Collard Greens

I still believe that greens are best cooked until they're really soft, and this recipe makes them flavorful too. Serve them with any Southern meal, especially if it includes fried chicken or pork chops.

Makes 6 to 8 servings | Prep time: 15 minutes | Minimum cook time: 2 hours in a medium slow cooker

2½ pounds collard greens

1 cup Vegetable Stock (page 24) or purchased stock

2 garlic cloves, minced

¼ cup cider vinegar

¼ cup granulated sugar

½ teaspoon dried thyme

1 bay leaf

Salt and red pepper flakes to taste

1. Rinse collard greens well, rubbing leaves to remove all grit and sand. Discard stems and cut leaves crosswise into ¹/₂-inch strips.

2. Bring stock, garlic, vinegar, sugar, and thyme to a boil in a large saucepan. Add as many greens as will fit into the pan by pushing greens into boiling liquid. Add more greens as those in the pan wilt. When all greens are wilted, pour greens into the slow cooker, and add bay leaf.

3. Cook on Low for 4 to 6 hours or on High for 2 to 3 hours, or until greens are very tender. Remove and discard bay leaf, season to taste with salt and red pepper flakes, and serve hot.

Note: The dish can be prepared up to 2 days in advance and refrigerated, tightly covered. Reheat it, covered, over low heat until hot, stirring occasionally.

Variation:

* Substitute kale or Swiss chard for the collard greens, and reduce the cooking time by 1 hour on Low or 30 minutes on High.

Greens were a mainstay of the poor Southern diet, and though the nutritional profile might not have been known at the time, it is certainly impressive. One serving of greens provides more than your daily requirement of vitamins C and A. Greens have a substantial amount of iron and calcium, fiber, and minerals. And they are one of the few good nondairy sources of calcium.

Hot German Potato Salad

The vinegar and mustard in this dish cut through the richness of game meats wonderfully, and it's also great with roasted pork, beef, or poultry.

Makes 6 to 8 servings | Prep time: 15 minutes | Minimum cook time: 4 hours in a medium slow cooker

¼ pound bacon, cut into 1-inch slices

¼ cup distilled white vinegar

2 tablespoons granulated sugar

2 tablespoons Dijon mustard

Salt and freshly ground black pepper to taste

4 large redskin potatoes, scrubbed and thinly sliced

1 large sweet onion, such as Vidalia or Bermuda, diced

3 tablespoons chopped fresh parsley

1. Cook bacon in a heavy skillet over medium-high heat for 5 to 7 minutes, or until crisp. Remove bacon from the pan with a slotted spoon, and set aside. Add ½ cup water, vinegar, sugar, mustard, salt, and pepper to the skillet, and stir well.

2. Arrange half of potato slices in the slow cooker, and top with half of onion. Repeat with remaining potatoes and onion. Pour dressing over vegetables. Cook on Low for 8 to 10 hours or on High for 4 to 5 hours, or until potatoes are tender. Stir in parsley and bacon, season to taste with salt and pepper, and serve hot.

Note: The dish can be prepared up to 2 days in advance and refrigerated, tightly covered. Reheat it, covered, in a 350°F oven for 20 to 25 minutes, or until hot.

Variation:

❋ Omit the bacon, and create a dressing with ⅓ cup olive oil.

> Dijon mustard, known for its clean, sharp flavor, was actually invented in Dijon, France. It is made from a combination of brown and black mustard seeds, and the essential ingredients are white wine and unfermented grape juice. Grey Poupon is a best-known brand in America, but there are dozens of French producers, many of which also flavor their mustard.

Herbed Tomato Sauce

Use this easy sauce to top grilled or broiled foods, or mix it with some browned chopped meat or Italian sausage and you've got a quickie pasta sauce.

Makes 2 pints | Prep time: 20 minutes | Minimum cook time: 4 hours in a medium slow cooker

¼ cup olive oil

1 large onion, chopped

½ red bell pepper, seeds and ribs removed, and chopped

2 garlic cloves, minced

1 (28-ounce) can crushed tomatoes

1 (6-ounce) can tomato paste

½ cup dry white wine

2 tablespoons chopped fresh oregano or 2 teaspoons dried

2 tablespoons chopped fresh basil or 2 teaspoons dried

1 tablespoon chopped fresh rosemary or 1 teaspoons dried

1 bay leaf

Salt and freshly ground black pepper to taste

1. Heat oil in a medium skillet over medium-high heat. Add onion, bell pepper, and garlic. Cook, stirring frequently, for 3 minutes, or until onion is translucent. Scrape the mixture into the slow cooker.

2. Add tomatoes, tomato paste, wine, ½ cup water, oregano, basil, rosemary, and bay leaf to the slow cooker, and stir well. Cook on Low for 6 to 8 hours or on High for 3 to 4 hours, or until vegetables are tender.

3. If cooking on Low, increase the heat to High. Cook sauce, uncovered, for 1 hour, stirring occasionally, or until slightly thickened. Remove and discard bay leaf, and season to taste with salt and pepper.

Note: The sauce can be prepared up to 4 days in advance and refrigerated, tightly covered. It can also be frozen for up to 3 months.

Variation:

❋ Substitute red wine for the white wine.

> For many recipes you only need a few tablespoons or a partial cup of tomato sauce, so why not freeze a batch in different sized containers? That way you'll know that the half pint container is 1 cup and a pint is 2 cups.

Gingered Barbecue Sauce

I encountered this barbecue sauce many years ago at a restaurant in Atlanta. The additions of fresh ginger and a sliced lemon add to both its aroma and flavor.

Makes 2 pints | Prep time: 10 minutes | Minimum cook time: 2 hours in a medium slow cooker

1 (20-ounce) bottle ketchup

1 cup cider vinegar

½ cup firmly packed dark brown sugar

5 tablespoons Worcestershire sauce

¼ cup vegetable oil

2 tablespoons dry mustard

2 garlic cloves, sliced

3 tablespoons thinly sliced fresh ginger

1 lemon, washed and thinly sliced

½ to 1 teaspoon hot red pepper sauce or to taste

1. Combine ketchup, vinegar, brown sugar, Worcestershire sauce, oil, mustard, garlic, ginger, and lemon in the slow cooker. Stir well.

2. Cook on Low for 4 to 6 hours or on High for 2 to 3 hours, or until sauce is bubbly. Season to taste with red pepper sauce.

3. Ladle sauce through a strainer, pressing with the back of a spoon to extract as much liquid as possible. Discard solids. Ladle sauce into containers, cover tightly, and refrigerate.

Note: The sauce can be prepared up to 1 week in advance and refrigerated, tightly covered. It can also be frozen for up to 3 months.

Variations:

✳ Substitute pure maple syrup for the brown sugar, and add 1 (3-inch) cinnamon stick to the slow cooker.

✳ Substitute rice wine vinegar for the cider vinegar, hoisin sauce for the brown sugar, omit the Worcestershire sauce, and add 1 teaspoon Chinese five-spice powder to the slow cooker.

> **Worcestershire sauce has been around for almost two centuries. It was first made in Worcester, England, by two pharmacists, or as they're called there "chemists," named John Wheeley Lea and William Henry Perrins in 1837. H.J. Heinz purchased Lea & Perrins in 2005, but the plant dating from 1897 in England is still in operation.**

Sweet Potatoes and Apples

This is a New England version of candied sweet potatoes, with applesauce and maple syrup providing moisture while cinnamon adds a bit of aroma and spice. Serve it with any simple roasted poultry or pork dish, and even with some game meats such as venison.

Makes 6 to 8 servings | *Prep time: 20 minutes* | *Minimum cook time: 3 hours in a medium slow cooker*

3 large sweet potatoes or yams
(about 3 pounds), peeled and thinly sliced

2 Granny Smith apples, peeled, cored, and thinly sliced

1 cup chunky applesauce

½ cup pure maple syrup

6 tablespoons unsalted butter, melted

¾ teaspoon ground cinnamon

Pinch of salt

Vegetable oil spray

1. Grease the inside of the slow cooker liberally with vegetable oil spray.

2. Arrange half of sweet potatoes and apples in the slow cooker. Combine applesauce, maple syrup, melted butter, cinnamon, and salt in a mixing bowl. Pour half of mixture over sweet potatoes and apples, and repeat with remaining sweet potatoes, apples, and applesauce mixture.

3. Cook on Low for 6 to 8 hours or on High for 3 to 4 hours, or until sweet potatoes are tender.

Note: The dish can be prepared up to 2 days in advance and refrigerated, tightly covered. Reheat it, covered, in a 350°F oven for 20 to 25 minutes, or until hot.

Variation:
* Substitute hoisin sauce for the maple syrup and Chinese five-spice powder for the cinnamon.

> Although sweet potatoes and yams are used interchangeably in recipes, they are different tubers. Yams are native to Africa and have a flesh that is lighter in color but sweeter than sweet potatoes. Yams also have a higher moisture content, so cut back slightly on liquids if you are using an authentic yam in a dish.

Chapter 9

Grand Finales:
Dessert Puddings and Fruity Treats

*f*inding options for the sweet ending to a meal is frequently a problem for those on a gluten-free diet. But that doesn't need to be the case, and the slow cooker is as much a friend in making luscious desserts as it is for all the courses that come before it.

There's a whole range of desserts that need some low-temperature simmering, which is what the slow cooker does best. These include homey puddings made from rice or gluten-free bread, as well as a range of fruit desserts. And then there are fondues; small slow cookers can do double duty as fondue pots.

If you have two slow cookers of different shapes, use the round one for desserts. I've found that oval slow cookers are wonderful for roasts, but round ones cook sweet custards more evenly. But worry not if the only slow cooker you have is oval. All of these recipes will still work well.

If you want a crispy cookie to go with one of these creamy desserts, you'll find many options for any time of the year in my book *Gluten-Free Christmas Cookies,* also published by Cider Mill Press.

Chocolate Pudding Cake

Pudding cakes are the quintessential slow cooker dessert. You start by pouring boiling water over a thick batter, and what you find a few hours later is a moist cake sitting on top of a thick sauce. I worked for many hours to make one with gluten-free products, and I now like it even better than the prototype made with wheat flour!

Makes 6 to 8 servings | Prep time: 15 minutes | Minimum cook time: 2 hours in a medium slow cooker

1 cup granulated sugar

¾ cup white rice flour

¼ cup cornstarch

½ cup unsweetened cocoa powder, divided

2 teaspoons gluten-free baking powder

¼ teaspoon salt

½ cup whole milk

5 tablespoons unsalted butter, melted

½ teaspoon pure vanilla extract

¾ cup firmly packed dark brown sugar

1¾ cups boiling water

1 pint of your favorite ice cream (optional)

Vegetable oil spray

1. Grease the inside of the slow cooker liberally with vegetable oil spray or melted butter. Combine granulated sugar, rice flour, cornstarch, ¼ cup cocoa, baking powder, and salt in a mixing bowl. Stir in milk, melted butter, and vanilla. Stir until a stiff batter forms. Spread batter into the slow cooker.

2. Sprinkle brown sugar and remaining ¼ cup cocoa powder over batter, then pour boiling water over batter. Cook on High for 2 to 2¼ hours, or until a toothpick inserted into the top cake layer comes out clean. Allow cake to sit for 15 minutes with slow cooker turned off before serving.

Note: The cake can be served hot, at room temperature, or chilled, topped with ice cream, if using.

Variations:
* Add 1 tablespoon instant coffee granules to the batter for a mocha cake.
* Add 2 tablespoon of any liqueur or liquor to the cake for added flavor.
* Add ¼ cup fruit-only jam to the batter for added flavor.
* Add ½ cup butterscotch chips to the batter for extra richness.
* Add ½ teaspoon ground cinnamon and ½ cup toasted slivered almonds to the batter for a Mexican chocolate combination.

> **Baking powder doesn't live forever. Mix 2 teaspoons of baking powder with 1 cup of hot tap water. If there's an immediate reaction of fizzing and foaming, the baking powder can be used. If the reaction is at all delayed or weak, throw the baking powder away and buy a fresh can.**

Indian Pudding

This thick and rich pudding is a wonderful fall or winter dessert, regardless of whether the meal is American or not. It's sweetened with a combination of maple syrup and brown sugar, and has some added interest from the inclusion of crystallized ginger.

Makes 6 to 8 servings | *Prep time: 30 minutes* | *Minimum cook time: 3 hours in a medium slow cooker*

5 cups whole milk

¾ cup firmly packed dark brown sugar

½ cup pure maple syrup

¾ cup yellow cornmeal

6 tablespoons unsalted butter, cut into small pieces

½ teaspoon pure vanilla extract

3 tablespoons finely chopped crystallized ginger

½ teaspoon salt

Caramel Sauce (page 249), optional

Vegetable oil spray

1. Combine milk, brown sugar, and maple syrup in a 2-quart saucepan, and stir well. Heat over medium heat, stirring occasionally, until mixture comes to a boil. Whisk in cornmeal, and simmer mixture, whisking frequently, for 10 minutes or until thick.

2. Stir butter and vanilla into mixture. Whisk until butter melts. Remove the pan from the heat, and stir in crystallized ginger and salt.

3. Grease the inside of the slow cooker liberally with vegetable oil spray or butter. Scrape mixture into the slow cooker. Cook on Low for 3 to 5 hours, or until the edges have darkened slightly and the center of pudding is set. Serve warm with caramel sauce, if using.

Note: The dish can be prepared up to 2 days in advance and refrigerated, tightly covered. Reheat it, covered, in a 350°F oven for 20 to 25 minutes, or until hot.

Because Native Americans introduced corn to the Pilgrims, anything made with corn had "Indian" as a prefix at one time or another. The other term for Indian Pudding is Hasty Pudding, and the Hasty Pudding Club at Harvard University, founded in 1770, was named for the dessert because it was eaten at the first meeting. Recipes for Indian or Hasty pudding go back to the early eighteenth century.

Baked Apples

The nuts form a textural contrast to the soft apples in this homey dessert. It's important to peel the top half of the apple. If you don't, the steam builds up inside the skin and the apple tends to fall apart.

Makes 4 servings | *Prep time: 15 minutes* | *Minimum cook time: 2 hours in a medium slow cooker*

4 baking apples, such as Jonathan and Northern Spy

2 tablespoons pure maple syrup

2 tablespoons unsalted butter, melted

¼ teaspoon ground cinnamon

¼ cup chopped walnuts

⅓ cup raisins

¼ cup rum

1. Core apples and peel the top half only. Place apples in the slow cooker. Combine maple syrup, melted butter, cinnamon, walnuts, and raisins in a small bowl. Spoon equal portions of the mixture into cores of apples. Spoon rum over apples.

2. Cook on Low for 4 to 6 hours or on High for 2 to 3 hours, or until apples are tender when pierced with the tip of a knife. Serve hot, at room temperature, or chilled.

Note: The apples can be prepared up to 2 days in advance and refrigerated, tightly covered.

Variation:

＊ Substitute crème de cassis for the rum, substitute granulated sugar for the maple syrup, and omit the cinnamon.

> The Jolly Green Giant and Aunt Jemima were created by ad agencies as fantasy product endorsers. But there certainly was a Johnny Appleseed. Born John Chapman in Massachusetts in 1774, he began to trek the countryside around 1800, planting apple trees in what were then the western territories. He's credited with planting thousands of apple trees before his death in 1845.

Orange Cranberry Rice Pudding

The combination of orange and cranberry is becoming a classic, from relishes and sauces on the Thanksgiving table to muffins and creamy rice pudding like this one. Top it with additional orange marmalade for an even richer dish.

Makes 4 to 6 servings | Prep time: 30 minutes | Minimum cook time: 2 hours in a medium slow cooker

1 cup converted long-grain rice

1 cup granulated sugar, divided

Salt to taste

1½ cups whole milk

½ cup orange marmalade

2 large eggs, lightly beaten

½ cup dried cranberries

1 cup heavy whipping cream

Vegetable oil spray

1. Place rice in a sieve, and rinse it well under cold water. Place rice in a 2-quart saucepan with 3 cups water, ½ cup sugar, and salt. Bring to a boil over high heat, and boil for 15 minutes, or until rice is tender. Drain rice.

2. Grease the inside of the slow cooker liberally with vegetable oil spray or butter. Spoon rice into the slow cooker. Combine milk, remaining ½ cup sugar, orange marmalade, and eggs in a mixing bowl, and whisk well. Stir mixture into rice, and add cranberries. Cook on Low for 4 to 5 hours or on High for 2 to 3 hours, or until custard is set.

3. Remove pudding from the slow cooker, and chill it well. When rice is chilled, place cream in a chilled mixing bowl. Whip cream with an electric mixer on medium until it thickens, then increase the speed to high, and whip cream until stiff peaks form. Fold whipped cream into rice. Serve immediately or refrigerate for up to 1 day, tightly covered with plastic wrap.

Note: The pudding can be made up to 1 day in advance and refrigerated, tightly covered.

Variation:
✱ Substitute lemon marmalade for the orange marmalade, and substitute dried blueberries for the cranberries.

The granulated sugar we take for granted today as a staple was once so rare and expensive it was called "white gold." Sugar cane, the first source of sugar, is a perennial grass that originated in Asia but is now grown in virtually every tropical and subtropical region of the world. It was only during the nineteenth century that refining beets for their sugar became commonplace.

Ibarra Chocolate Rice Pudding

The type of chocolate most popular in Mexico is a grainy block used to make hot chocolate. The most famous brand is Ibarra, and all Mexican chocolate contains both ground almonds and cinnamon, so they're the additions to this pudding.

Makes 4 to 6 servings | Prep time: 15 minutes | Minimum cook time: 2 1/2 hours in a medium slow cooker

1 cup slivered blanched almonds

1 cup Arborio rice

3 cups half-and-half

1 (14-ounce) can sweetened condensed milk

1/4 cup Amaretto

6 ounces good quality bittersweet chocolate, chopped

1/2 teaspoon ground cinnamon

Pinch of salt

1/2 cup heavy whipping cream

Vanilla ice cream or sweetened whipped cream (optional)

Vegetable oil spray

1. Preheat the oven to 350°F. Place almonds on a baking sheet and toast for 5 to 7 minutes, or until browned. Remove nuts from the oven, chop coarsely, and set aside. Rinse the rice well under cold running water.

2. Grease the inside of the slow cooker liberally with vegetable oil spray or butter. Combine rice, half-and-half, sweetened condensed milk, Amaretto, chocolate, cinnamon, and salt in the slow cooker. Stir well.

3. Cook on Low for 5 to 7 hours or on High for 2 1/2 to 3 hours, or until rice is soft and the liquid is thick. Stir in heavy cream. Serve hot, warm, or chilled, topped with ice cream or whipped cream, if using.

Note: The pudding can be made up to 1 day in advance and refrigerated, tightly covered.

Variation:

* Substitute white chocolate for the dark chocolate, and substitute Grand Marnier for the Amaretto. Omit the cinnamon, and add 1 tablespoon grated orange zest to the slow cooker.

> All white rice has some starch on the surface; with Asian rice this is even more of a problem because the starch is used as a preservative. That's why it's important to rinse the rice if specified in a recipe. Otherwise it can become gummy.

Pineapple-Coconut Bread Pudding

This bread pudding has all the luscious flavors of drinking a piña colada; it's laced with coconut and pineapple and scented with rum.

Makes 6 to 8 servings | Prep time: 15 minutes | Minimum cook time: 3 hours in a medium slow cooker

5 large eggs

½ cup granulated sugar

1½ cups whole milk

1 (15-ounce) can cream of coconut, such as Coco López

1 (8-ounce) can crushed pineapple, undrained

6 tablespoons (¾ stick) unsalted butter, melted

¼ cup rum (or 1 teaspoon rum extract plus ¼ cup water)

½ teaspoon pure vanilla extract

Pinch of salt

½ pound loaf gluten-free French or Italian bread, cut into ½-inch slices

Vegetable oil spray

1. Combine eggs, sugar, milk, cream of coconut, pineapple, butter, rum, vanilla, and salt in a mixing bowl, and whisk well. Add bread slices to the mixing bowl, and press them down so that bread will absorb liquid. Allow mixture to sit for 10 minutes.

2. Grease the inside of the slow cooker liberally with vegetable oil spray or melted butter. Spoon mixture into the slow cooker.

3. Cook on High for 1 hour, then reduce the heat to Low and cook for 2 to 3 hours, or until puffed and an instant-read thermometer inserted in the center registers 165°F. Serve hot or at room temperature.

Note: The bread pudding can be baked up to 2 days in advance and refrigerated, tightly covered. Reheat it in a 325°F oven, covered, for 15 to 20 minutes, or until warm.

The best place to store eggs is in their cardboard carton. The carton helps prevent moisture loss, and it shields the eggs from absorbing odors from other foods. If you're not sure if your eggs are fresh, submerge them in a bowl of cool water. If they stay on the bottom, they're fine. If they float to the top, it shows they're old because eggs develop an air pocket at one end as they age.

Coconut Ginger Rice Pudding

Rice pudding is part of Asian cuisines too, and I've discovered that the plump grains of Arborio rice used for savory dishes such as risotto make great rice pudding with Asian flavors too. This is a wonderful way to end an Asian meal!

Makes 6 to 8 servings | Prep time: 15 minutes | Minimum cook time: 2 1/2 hours in a medium slow cooker

1 cup Arborio rice

1 (14-ounce) can unsweetened coconut milk

1 (14-ounce) can sweetened condensed milk

2 cups half-and-half

½ cup finely chopped crystallized ginger

½ teaspoon ground cinnamon

¼ teaspoon salt

½ cup heavy whipping cream

Vegetable oil spray

Chopped fresh mango or pineapple (optional)

1. Grease the inside of the slow cooker liberally with vegetable oil spray or butter. Combine rice, coconut milk, sweetened condensed milk, half-and-half, ginger, cinnamon, and salt in the slow cooker. Stir well.

2. Cook on Low for 5 to 7 hours or on High for 2½ to 3 hours, or until rice is soft and the liquid is thick. Stir in heavy cream. Serve hot, warm, or chilled, topped with chopped fruit, if using.

Note: The pudding can be made up to 1 day in advance and refrigerated, tightly covered.

Crystallized ginger is fresh ginger that is candied in sugar syrup and then tossed with coarse sugar as a way to preserve it. Its flavor is like a more mellow fresh ginger than the harshness of ground ginger. It's very expensive in little bottles in the spice aisle, but most whole foods markets sell it in bulk.

Chocolate Fondue

Few dishes are as universally popular with all generations as gooey chocolate fondue. It's a snap to make and you can cut up the foods for dipping as the chocolate melts.

Makes 6 to 8 servings | *Prep time: 10 minutes* | *Minimum cook time: 45 minutes in a 1-quart slow cooker*

¾ pound good-quality bittersweet chocolate, chopped

½ cup heavy whipping cream

3 tablespoons liqueur or liquor (your favorite: rum, bourbon, tequila, Cognac, brandy, triple sec, Grand Marnier, Chambord, kirsch, Amaretto, Frangelico, crème de cacao, crème de banana, Irish cream liqueur, Kahlúa)

1. Combine chocolate, cream, and liqueur in the slow cooker. Cook on Low for 45 to 60 minutes, or until chocolate melts. Stir gently toward the end of the cooking time.

2. Serve directly from the slow cooker with hulled strawberries (halved if large), banana chunks, clementine segments, apple slices, cubes of gluten-free cakes or cookies, or meringue cookies.

Note: The fondue can be prepared up to 6 hours in advance and kept in the slow cooker. Reheat it until hot before serving.

One of the additional health benefits of chocolate is that it has been found to contain catechins—some of the same antioxidants found in green tea. The catechins attack free radicals that damage cells and are thought to lead to cancer and heart disease. Therefore, eating chocolate may help to prevent heart disease and cancer—as long as it's eaten in small quantities.

Bittersweet Chocolate Coconut Cream Fondue

This fondue reminds me of munching a Mounds bar, which is one of my favorite candies, because it includes rich chocolate balanced with coconut. And then there's a shot of rum in it too. What could be better?

Makes 6 to 8 servings | Prep time: 10 minutes | Minimum cook time: 45 minutes in a 1-quart slow cooker

9 ounce bittersweet chocolate, chopped

1 ounce unsweetened chocolate, chopped

1 cup sweetened cream of coconut (such as Coco López)

½ cup heavy whipping cream

¼ cup dark rum

¼ teaspoon pure coconut extract

1. Combine bittersweet chocolate, unsweetened chocolate, cream of coconut, cream, rum, and coconut extract in the slow cooker. Cook on Low for 45 to 60 minutes, or until chocolates melt. Stir gently toward the end of the cooking time.

2. Serve directly from the slow cooker with hulled strawberries (halved if large), banana chunks, clementine segments, apple slices, cubes of gluten-free cakes or cookies, or meringue cookies.

Note: The fondue can be prepared up to 6 hours in advance and kept in the slow cooker. Reheat it until hot before serving.

Variation:

✳ If you want to turn the fondue into a variation on Almond Joy, add ¹⁄₂ cup chopped toasted almonds to it.

Cream of coconut is not the same as coconut milk. This is a gluten-free and highly-sweetened thick mixture made basically from coconut and sugar. Do not substitute coconut milk for it. Cream of coconut might be found with the drink mixers, such as Bloody Mary mix, rather than in the baking aisle.

Apple Crumble

The wonderful news is that oats, which make up much of crumble topping, are gluten-free, and sweet rice flour takes the place of wheat flour in this yummy fall dessert scented with cinnamon and ginger.

Makes 4 to 6 servings | Prep time: 15 minutes | Minimum cook time: 1 1/2 hours in a medium slow cooker

¼ pound (1 stick) unsalted butter

2 pounds Granny Smith apples, cored and thinly sliced (and peeled, if desired)

2 tablespoons freshly squeezed lemon juice

¼ cup granulated sugar

2 tablespoons sweet rice flour

1 teaspoon ground cinnamon, divided

½ teaspoon ground ginger

Pinch of salt

¾ cup gluten-free oats

½ cup firmly packed dark brown sugar

Vanilla ice cream or sweetened whipped cream for serving (optional)

1. Cut 2 tablespoons butter into small bits, and set aside. Melt remaining 6 tablespoons butter, and set aside.

2. Place apples in the slow cooker and toss with lemon juice. Mix granulated sugar, rice flour, 1/2 teaspoon cinnamon, ginger, and salt in a small bowl. Toss apples with mixture, and spread apples into an even layer. Dot top of apples with butter bits.

3. Mix oats with brown sugar, remaining cinnamon, and melted butter in a small mixing bowl. Sprinkle topping over apples. Cook on Low for 3 to 4 hours or on High for 1 1/2 to 2 hours, or until apples are soft. Serve hot or warm, topped with ice cream or whipped cream, if using.

Note: The dish can be prepared up to 2 days in advance and refrigerated, tightly covered. Reheat it, covered, in a 350°F oven for 20 to 25 minutes, or until hot.

Variations:

❋ Add 1/2 cup raisins, dried cranberries, or chopped dried apricots to the apples.

❋ Omit the cinnamon, substitute granulated sugar for the brown sugar, and add 2 tablespoons grated orange zest to the topping.

> It's important to use fresh rather than bottled lemon juice to prevent fruits from undergoing oxidation. Most bottled lemon juices aren't strong enough, but you can always use lime juice if you're out of lemon.

Pears Poached in Red Wine

Poached pears are an elegant way to end a meal, and in this version their fruitiness is amplified by using crème de cassis balanced with citrus zest.

Makes 4 to 6 servings | Prep time: 15 minutes | Minimum cook time: 1½ hours in a medium slow cooker

4 to 6 ripe pears, peeled, halved, and cored
2 cups dry red wine
¼ cup crème de cassis
½ cup granulated sugar
1 (3-inch) cinnamon stick
1 (3-inch) strip lemon zest
1 (3-inch) strip orange zest

1. Arrange pears in the slow cooker; cut them into quarters, if necessary, to make them fit. Combine wine, crème de cassis, and sugar in a mixing bowl. Stir well to dissolve sugar, and pour mixture over pears. Add cinnamon stick, lemon zest, and orange zest to the slow cooker.

2. Cook on Low for 3 to 4 hours or on High for 1½ to 2 hours, or until pears are tender when pierced with the point of a knife.

3. Remove pears from the slow cooker with a slotted spoon, and arrange them in a serving dish. Strain the red wine mixture into a saucepan, discarding the solids. Bring the liquid to a boil over high heat, and cook until reduced by half, stirring occasionally. Pour reduced liquid over pears, and serve pears at room temperature or chilled.

Note: The pears can be poached up to 2 days in advance and refrigerated, tightly covered.

Variations:
* Substitute dry white wine for the red wine, and substitute 3 slices fresh ginger the size of a quarter for the cinnamon stick.
* Substitute fresh peaches, peeled and stoned, for the pears.

> An easy way to core halved pears and apples is with a melon baller. The shape is efficient, and it leaves a neatly formed round hole. Another choice is a serrated grapefruit spoon.

Classic New Orleans Bread Pudding

Bread puddings and French toast were devised centuries ago as a way to utilize stale bread, and there are now so many gluten-free breads on the market that you may end up with some leftovers. The slow cooker makes great bread puddings that puff almost like a soufflé.

Makes 6 to 8 servings | Prep time: 15 minutes | Minimum cook time: 3 hours in a medium slow cooker

½ cup raisins

¼ cup bourbon

½ cup chopped pecans

5 large eggs

1 cup granulated sugar

2 cups whole milk

6 tablespoons (¾ stick) unsalted butter, melted

1½ teaspoons pure vanilla extract

1 teaspoon ground cinnamon

Pinch of salt

½ pound loaf gluten-free French or Italian bread, cut into ½-inch slices

½ to ¾ cup Caramel Sauce (page 249) or commercial caramel sauce

Vegetable oil spray

1. Preheat the oven to 350°F. Combine raisins and rum in a microwave-safe dish, and microwave on High (100 percent power) for 40 seconds. Place pecans on a baking sheet and toast for 5 to 7 minutes, or until browned. Set aside.

2. Combine eggs, sugar, milk, melted butter, vanilla, cinnamon, and salt in a mixing bowl, and whisk well. Add bread slices to the mixing bowl, and press them down so that bread will absorb liquid. Stir in raisins and pecans. Allow mixture to sit for 10 minutes.

3. Grease the inside of the slow cooker liberally with vegetable oil spray or melted butter. Spoon mixture into the slow cooker.

4. Cook on High for 1 hour, then reduce the heat to Low and cook for 2 to 3 hours, or until puffed and an instant-read thermometer inserted in the center registers 165°F. Serve hot or at room temperature, topped with caramel sauce.

Note: The bread pudding can be baked up to 2 days in advance and refrigerated, tightly covered. Reheat it in a 325°F oven, covered, for 15 to 20 minutes, or until warm.

Variations:

✳ Omit the sugar, cinnamon and pecans, and add 1½ cups white chocolate, melted, to the bread mixture. Serve with chocolate sauce.

✳ Substitute maple syrup for the granulated sugar, reduce the cinnamon to ½ teaspoon, and substitute walnuts for the pecans.

✳ Substitute ¾ cup orange marmalade for ¾ cup of the sugar, omit the cinnamon and pecans, and substitute dried cranberries for the raisins. Serve topped with ice cream or sweetened whipped cream.

Vegetable oil spray has a tendency to coat the counter as well as the inside of the slow cooker, so here's a trick to contain it: Open the dishwasher door, place the slow cooker insert right on the door, and spray away. Any excess or overspray will be cleaned off the door the next time you run the dishwasher.

Caramel Sauce

Caramel is simply sugar and water cooked to a high temperature, and once that's done just add some butter and cream you've got caramel sauce.

Makes about 1¹/₂ cups | Prep time: 5 minutes | Start to finish: 15 minutes

1½ cups granulated sugar

¼ teaspoon kosher salt

4 tablespoons (½ stick) unsalted butter, cut into small pieces

1 cup heavy whipping cream

1 teaspoon pure vanilla extract

1. Combine sugar, salt, and 1 cup of water in a saucepan, and bring to a boil over medium-high heat. Swirl the pan by the handle but do not stir. Raise the heat to high, and allow syrup to cook until it reaches a walnut brown color, swirling the pot by the handle frequently.

2. Remove the pan from the heat, and stir in butter and cream with a long-handled spoon. (The mixture will bubble furiously at first.) Return the pan to low heat and stir until any lumps melt and the sauce is smooth. Stir in vanilla, and transfer to a jar. Serve hot, room temperature, or cold.

Note: The sauce can be refrigerated for up to 1 week.

Variation:
✳ Reduce the vanilla to ¹/₂ teaspoon and add 2 tablespoons of brandy, rum, or a liqueur to the sauce.

> The easiest way to clean a pan in which you've caramelized sugar or made caramel sauce is to fill the pan with water and place it back on the stove. Stir as the water comes to a boil and the pan will be virtually clean.

Common Weights and Measures

Table of Weights and Measures of Common Ingredients

FOOD	QUANTITY	YIELD
Apples	1 pound	2 $\frac{1}{2}$ to 3 cups sliced
Avocado	1 pound	1 cup mashed fruit
Bananas	1 medium	1 cup, sliced
Bell Peppers	1 pound	3 to 4 cups sliced
Blueberries	1 pound	3 $\frac{1}{3}$ cups
Butter	$\frac{1}{4}$ pound (1 stick)	8 tablespoons
Cabbage	1 pound	4 cups packed shredded
Carrots	1 pound	3 cups diced or sliced
Chocolate, morsels	12 ounces	2 cups
Chocolate, bulk	1 ounce	3 tablespoons grated
Cocoa powder	1 ounces	$\frac{1}{4}$ cup
Coconut, flaked	7 ounces	2 $\frac{1}{2}$ cups
Cream, heavy	$\frac{1}{2}$ pint	1 cup, 2 cups whipped
Cream cheese	8 ounces	1 cup
Flour, rice	1 pound	4 cups
Lemons	1 medium	3 tablespoons juice
Lemons	1 medium	2 teaspoons zest
Milk	1 quart	4 cups
Molasses	12 ounces	1 $\frac{1}{2}$ cups
Mushrooms	1 pound	5 cups sliced
Onions	1 medium	$\frac{1}{2}$ cup chopped

Peaches	1 pound	2 cups sliced
Peanuts	5 ounces	1 cup
Pecans	6 ounces	$1\frac{1}{2}$ cups
Pineapple	1 medium	3 cups diced fruit
Potatoes	1 pound	3 cups sliced
Raisins	1 pound	3 cups
Rice	1 pound	2 to $2\frac{1}{2}$ cups raw
Spinach	1 pound	$\frac{3}{4}$ cup cooked
Squash, summer	1 pound	$3\frac{1}{2}$ cups sliced
Strawberries	1 pint	$1\frac{1}{2}$ cups sliced
Sugar, brown	1 pound	$2\frac{1}{4}$ cups, packed
Sugar, confectioner's	1 pound	4 cups
Sugar, granulated	1 pound	$2\frac{1}{4}$ cups
Tomatoes	1 pound	$1\frac{1}{2}$ cups pulp
Walnuts	4 ounces	1 cup

Table of Liquid Measurements

Pinch	=	less than $\frac{1}{8}$ teaspoon
3 teaspoons	=	1 tablespoon
2 tablespoons	=	1 ounces
8 tablespoons	=	$\frac{1}{2}$ cup
2 cups	=	1 pint
1 quart	=	2 pints
1 gallon	=	4 quarts

Metric Conversion Chart

The scientifically precise calculations needed for baking are not necessary when cooking conventionally. This chart is designed for general cooking. If making conversions for baking, grab your calculator and compute the exact figure.

Converting Ounces to Grams

The numbers in the following table are approximate. To reach the exact amount of grams, multiply the number of ounces by 28.35.

OUNCES	GRAMS
1 ounce	30 grams
2 ounces	60 grams
3 ounces	85 grams
4 ounces	115 grams
5 ounces	140 grams
6 ounces	180 grams
7 ounces	200 grams
8 ounces	225 grams
9 ounces	250 grams
10 ounces	285 grams
11 ounces	300 grams
12 ounces	340 grams
13 ounces	370 grams
14 ounces	400 grams
15 ounces	425 grams
16 ounces	450 grams

Converting Quarts to Liters

The numbers in the following table are approximate. To reach the exact amount of liters, multiply the number of quarts by 0.95.

QUARTS	LITER
1 cup ($1/4$ quart)	$1/4$ liter
1 pint ($1/2$ quart)	$1/2$ liter
1 quart	1 liter
2 quarts	2 liters
$2 1/2$ quarts	$2 1/2$ liters
3 quarts	$2 3/4$ liters
4 quarts	$3 3/4$ liters
5 quarts	$4 3/4$ liters
6 quarts	$5 1/2$ liters
7 quarts	$6 1/2$ liters
8 quarts	$7 1/2$ liters

Converting Pounds to Grams and Kilograms

The numbers in the following table are approximate. To reach the exact amount of kilograms, multiply the number of pounds by 453.6.

POUNDS	GRAMS; KILOGRAMS
1 pound	450 grams
1 1/2 pounds	675 grams
2 pounds	900 grams
2 1/2 pounds	1,125 grams; 1 1/4 kilograms
3 pounds	1,350 grams
3 1/2 pounds	1,500 grams; 1 1/2 kilograms
4 pounds	1,800 grams
4 1/2 pounds	2 kilograms
5 pounds	2 1/4 kilograms
5 1/2 pounds	2 1/2 kilograms
6 pounds	2 3/4 kilograms
6 1/2 pounds	3 kilograms
7 pounds	3 1/4 kilograms
7 1/2 pounds	3 1/2 kilograms
8 pounds	3 3/4 kilograms

Converting Fahrenheit to Celsius

The numbers in the following table are approximate. To reach the exact temperature, subtract 32 from the Fahrenheit reading, multiply the number by 5, then divide by 9.

FAHRENHEIT	CELSIUS
170	77
180	82
190	88
200	95
225	110
250	120
300	150
325	165
350	180
375	190
400	205
425	220
450	230
475	245
500	260

Index

About Cider Mill Press
Book Publishers

Good ideas ripen with time. From seed to harvest, Cider Mill Press brings fine reading, information, and entertainment together between the covers of its creatively crafted books. Our Cider Mill bears fruit twice a year, publishing a new crop of titles each spring and fall.

Visit us on the Web at
www.cidermillpress.com
or write to us at
12 Port Farm Road
Kennebunkport, Maine 04046